SPYDLE

SPYDLE

THE NATIONAL ARCHIVES, UK WITH

DR. GARETH MOORE AND
LAURA JAYNE AYRES

TEN SPEED PRESS
California | New York

Ten Speed Press
An imprint of the Crown Publishing Group
A division of Penguin Random House LLC
tenspeed.com

2024 Ten Speed Press Trade Paperback Edition

Text provided by The National Archives copyright © 2024 Crown Copyright
Puzzles copyright © 2024 by Any Puzzle Media Ltd.

Unless otherwise indicated all images Crown Copyright;
reproduced by permission of The National Archives, London England
Historical content compiled and written by Ela Kaczmarska and Timothy Cross

Ten Speed Press and the Ten Speed Press colophon are registered trademarks of
Penguin Random House LLC.

Set in Adobe Jeson and Futura
Designed and typeset by Couper Street Type Co.

ISBN 978-0-593-83770-2
Ebook ISBN 978-0-593-83771-9

Originally published in trade paperback in the United Kingdom by Penguin Book,
a division of Penguin Random House UK, in 2024.

Editor: Thea Diklich-Newell | Production editor: Ashley Pierce
Production designer: Mari Gill | Managing Editor: Kristin Sargianis
Production manager: Dan Myers
Proofreader: Tracy Lynch
Marketer: Chantelle Walker

Manufactured in The United States

1st Printing

First American Edition

Cover images © Shutterstock

CONTENTS

INTRODUCTION

The words 'secret intelligence' and 'espionage' often bring to mind the shadowy world of Cold War intrigue inhabited by James Bond in the Ian Fleming novels. The fictional British Secret Service agent is aided in his daring exploits by gadgets supplied by Q Branch, such as the infamous booby-trapped attaché case. This incredible device was, in fact, a real invention from the Second World War and was primed to explode when the lid was opened. Fleming himself worked in British naval intelligence and conceived Operation Goldeneye, a wartime plan to spy on General Franco's Spain, so it is unsurprising that his wartime experiences gave inspiration to his novels.

The stories unearthed at The National Archives and featured in this book span five hundred years of spying, from Henry VIII to the Cold War. They include the Gunpowder Plot to blow up Parliament in 1605, which was foiled thanks to a piece of last-minute intelligence. The threat of foreign invasion was kept at bay, traitors apprehended, diplomacy conducted and wars fought — all with the aid of spies.

What these stories show is that the motives and methods of spying are surprisingly enduring. The need to understand an adversary's capability can be seen both in the intelligence on the Spanish Armada, sent to invade Elizabeth I's England in 1588, but also in the monitoring of Soviet military deployments in East Germany in the 1980s. Ciphers were used by Mary, Queen of Scots, to encrypt her letters in a treasonous plot in 1586 to supplant Elizabeth I. Hundreds of years later, the cracking of the German Enigma codes – used to encrypt military communications – would prove vital to Allied victory in the Second World War. Invisible ink was as useful a tool in the First World War as it had been during the Gunpowder Plot.

The true story of espionage is as extraordinary as fiction, and it begins hundreds of years ago . . .

1 EARLY INTELLIGENCE

Kings were expected to hide their thinking from all but their closest advisers, partly because household spies were an accepted fact of elite life in the past. Even if it only resulted in gossip and did not cause a political crisis, monarchs required their officials to keep secret any knowledge that touched the wellbeing of the king or the health of the realm. Kings and queens had their spies listening into conversations from all manners of hiding places. Letters also contained secrets and were often intercepted.

Codes and ciphers were widely used by political rulers in sixteenth-century Europe. Monarchs, ministers and ambassadors often established cipher offices and employed cipher secretaries to encrypt diplomatic or military information. Mary, Queen of Scots, had a cipher secretary handle her 'secret' correspondence to communicate with her supporters while she was imprisoned in England. However, the encrypted messages were not as secure as she hoped.

Queen Elizabeth faced a constant threat from her enemies in England and Europe. Anti-Catholic laws created a climate of fear. The Catholic Mass was banned, those who would not attend Church of England services were fined or imprisoned, lands were confiscated, and to harbour Catholic priests was deemed treasonable. Sir Francis Walsingham, Elizabeth's Secretary of State, began recruiting spies from Oxford and Cambridge Universities and established the first known school of espionage in England. The exiled Roman Catholic spy Antony Standen passed information from Europe to Walsingham. His intelligence reports on the Spanish Armada made him a key figure in the Elizabethan secret service. He returned to England after nearly forty years in exile but his loyalty to his religion over the service to his country resulted in his imprisonment in the Tower of London.

Conspiracies to overthrow Elizabeth were uncovered by Walsingham's men throughout her reign. From 1571 to 1586 the discovery of a series of plots to establish Mary, Queen of Scots, on the throne led to the trial and execution of Mary and many of her friends and allies.

The State Papers at The National Archives are full of letters from informers and accounts of interrogations and searches.

1: THE BAG OF SECRETS

The *Baga de Secretis* was a repository for the records of some of the most important, sensational, constitutional state trials. Lasting for the next three centuries, this 'Bag of Secrets' – named after the original oxhide pouch that was used, and succeeded by a locked closet – contained intelligence or evidence of high-profile traitors obtained by espionage, including the Gunpowder plotters, those plotting to place usurpers such as Mary, Queen of Scots, on the throne, and the regicides who had condemned King Charles I for treason; its multiple locks kept its contents safe from prying eyes.

Illustration of Charles I on coram rege rolls that detailed court proceedings of the Court of King's Bench.

SPYDLE CHALLENGE

Reveal the name of the English royal (4, 6) whose trial documents were once kept in the *Baga de Secretis*. Jumbled up in the bag below are the letters of this unfortunate person's name, which can be formed using each letter exactly once.

Once you have found the hidden royal, how many regular English words can you find that can be spelled using the centre letter plus two or more of the other letters? No letter may be used more times than it appears within the circle. Targets: 20 words (good); 25 words (excellent).

2: HIDDEN HEARINGS

The fortress network around the English territory of Calais was a key outpost for trade and the projection of England's political influence. Struggling to keep control and in ill health, King Henry VII wanted to know what his chief officials in the garrison and town felt about the prospects for the Tudor dynasty keeping the crown. In September 1504, John Flamank, a royal agent, hid in a cupboard in the treasurer of Calais's house to discover what they were talking about. He overheard and recorded a discussion full of potential disloyalty, dangerous self-interest, speculation on the succession of the crown, and of growing tension at the top of a vulnerable regime.

Flamank's lengthy intelligence report was quickly sent to the king. It represents a rare survival of the kind of political information that we know was circulating within the government at Westminster across the medieval and early modern periods.

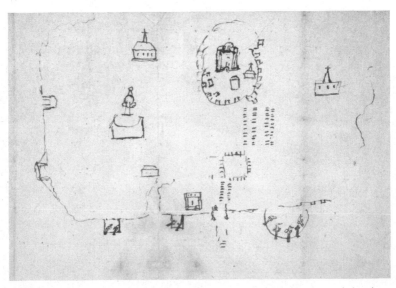

Rough plan of Calais from the 1500s, showing citadel, batteries, gates and churches.

SPYDLE CHALLENGE

Imagine you are recording the activities of three royal spies posted in European cities, and trying to understand which spy has heard what about the monarchy – and from inside which hiding place. Use your skills of logical deduction, along with the chart and table, to work out where each spy heard what snippet of gossip, both with respect to which city they were in and at what clandestine spot.

- The story overheard from a lavatory did not take place in Porto
- The rumour that the queen is unfaithful did not originate in Seville, nor was it acquired by hiding in a wardrobe
- Porto was not the place where a spy hid in a pantry
- The story that the new king is weak was overheard from a lavatory

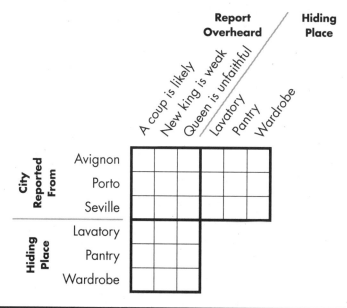

City Reported From	Report Overheard	Hiding Place

3: TUDOR TROUBLE

In an open diplomatic letter sent in Latin on 1 November 1509, eighteen-year-old Henry VIII of England was rebuked by his father-in-law, the much more experienced King Ferdinand of Aragon, for stating his strategic thinking towards France and Venice. At the end of the month, Ferdinand wrote in cipher to his daughter Queen Catherine, who was acting as his temporary ambassador, stressing the importance of discretion.

Henry VIII depicted in the Court of King's Bench coram rege *rolls.*

SPYDLE CHALLENGE

What was the warning that Ferdinand sent to his daughter? It has been disguised and left up to you to work out exactly what it was.

'Ycerces si yrassecen

ni taerg sesirpretne dna

taht gnihton dluohs eb

nettirw tpecxe ni rehpic'

4: VENETIAN SECRETS

Interception and coding/decoding of correspondence – and disguising it – were universal aspects of Renaissance diplomacy. The Venetian Ambassador, Andrea Badoer, who was in England from 1509 to 1515, revealed that he knew his correspondence was being opened – most likely by Thomas Wolsey.

Thomas Wolsey was a clergyman, royal chaplain and king's almoner (responsible for distributing alms to the poor). He quickly took control of England's diplomacy as Henry VIII sought to re-start war with France. Wolsey's expert bureaucratic brain and capacity to retain and manipulate information made him an ideal spymaster.

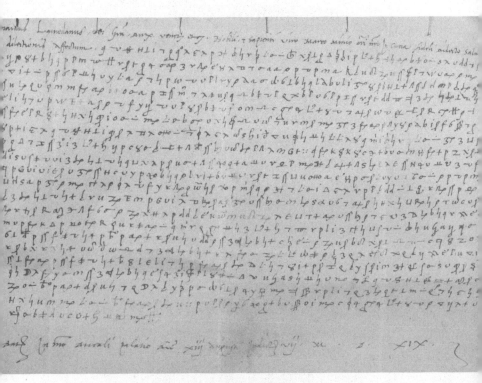

Early sixteenth-century Venetian correspondence in code.

SPYDLE CHALLENGE

Use your code-cracking skills to decipher the names of these ten historical Italian city-states, whose names have been disguised in the same way.

SELIRNU

GEITE

GINUE

ENCUNE

SOINE

POSE

EMELFO

REGASE

NULO

CELEBROE

As an extra challenge, how would the city of VENICE appear if encoded in the same way?

5: A CUNNING DISGUISE

England captured the French city of Tournai in the war of 1513, and it was run as an English outpost, even sending Members of Pariament (MPs) to the Westminster parliament. In April 1517, the Ambassador to France, Sir Richard Jerningham, received a letter from the king's council instructing him to 'set spies upon the French'. He then wrote to the governors of Tournai with news on what he planned to do.

Jerningham had two men already in the French king's court at Paris. He had already sent three more into Normandy. With rumours that German troops were ending their occupation of the Champagne region, he sent two linguists disguised as merchants – Robert van Claise and Thomas Lewis – to find out what was happening. They spoke to the captain of the German troops and sent back a full report on the movements. Another spy also passed on information on problems with Swiss mercenaries serving the French, and the news that many more had been recruited for a planned attack on Tournai.

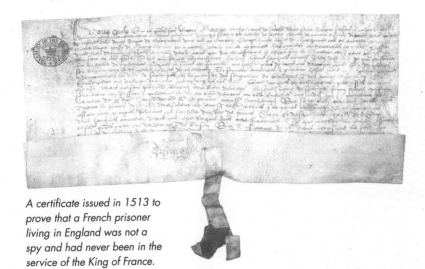

A certificate issued in 1513 to prove that a French prisoner living in England was not a spy and had never been in the service of the King of France.

SPYDLE CHALLENGE

Imagine you are coordinating a team of spies to be sent abroad, each disguised as a merchant of some kind, each speaking a different language and posted to a different French city. Use your deductive skills to work out where each spy is being sent, speaking what language, and with which faked goods.

- The spy conversing in French is either in Marseille or is selling spices – but not both
- The French-speaker is not in Annecy
- The spy speaking Dutch is either in Rouen or is the spice merchant – but not both
- Jewellery is not the ware being sold by the spy speaking French
- Flemish is not the language spoken by the jewellery merchant

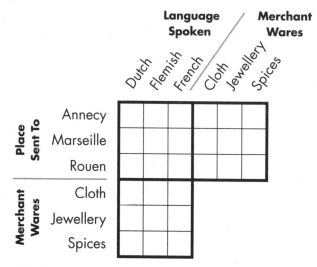

Place Sent To	Language Spoken	Merchant Wares

6: EXPENSIVE ASSETS

Henry VIII's war with France and Scotland from 1512 to 1513 cost a huge amount of money and spying played a large part in war preparations. Right at the start of Henry VIII's reign, in September 1509, the deputy Lieutenant of Calais, Sir Gilbert Talbot, was given a large sum for 'spyall money'. This became a regular payment in his budget.

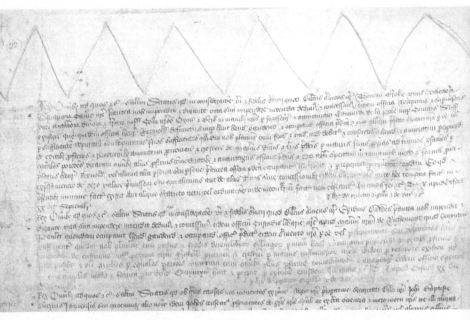

A record of spyall money payment.

SPYDLE CHALLENGE

Reveal the initial sum given to Sir Gilbert Talbot, in pounds. To calculate it, start with the number at the top of the chain, then follow the arrows to apply each operation in turn until you reach the 'TOTAL' box, writing your answer at the bottom. As part of the Spydle challenge, try to do the entire calculation in your head without writing anything down until you reach the final TOTAL area.

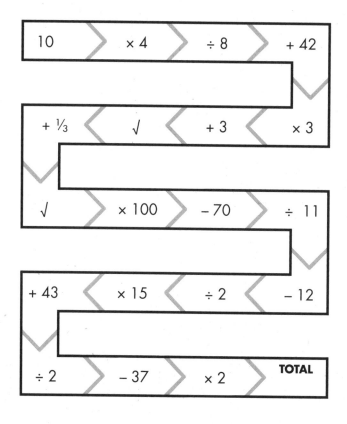

10	× 4	÷ 8	+ 42
+ ⅓	√	+ 3	× 3
√	× 100	− 70	÷ 11
+ 43	× 15	÷ 2	− 12
÷ 2	− 37	× 2	**TOTAL**

7: SPINELLY'S SPY

Early in Henry VIII's reign, letters from Sir Thomas Spinelly, the resident ambassador and spy in Antwerp, show the range of information he was able to gather. This included ship movements, arrivals and departures of people and copies of letters. He was also able to mobilise spies in other locations to follow trails.

A year earlier, in early 1513, Spinelly sent a man called Joes Pierdux on a coastal journey from Veer in Flanders to Brest in western France. He recorded the number of the French king's ships of war in each major harbour, and even noted where Scottish vessels were anchored. The resulting report was sent to Henry VIII on 21 March 1513.

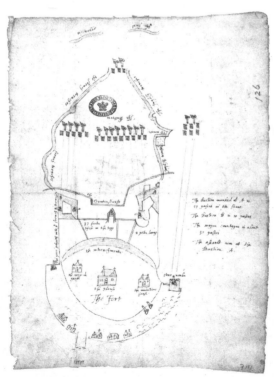

A sixteenth-century sketch of Crozon Fort, near Brest.

SPYDLE CHALLENGE

Imagine you are receiving reports from a spy abroad about the European coastal ports they have visited on a particular mission, and need to organise the stack of reports into the order they were visited. You know that eight ports were visited in total. You also know that:

- Cascais was visited before, but not immediately before, Bilbao
- Brest was the last port visited
- Bayonne was visited immediately before Brest
- Cascais was visited at some point between Cadiz and Oporto, although not necessarily in that order
- After Peniche was visited, one more port was visited before the spy then went to Bilbao
- Faro was visited immediately after Cadiz

Number each port with the order in which it was visited (writing '1' for the first port, '2' for the second, and so on):

Bayonne	☐	Cascais	☐
Bilbao	☐	Faro	☐
Brest	☐	Oporto	☐
Cadiz	☐	Peniche	☐

8: SPIES AND SUSPICIONS

In the lead-up to the Reformation, in which Henry VIII established the Church of England, Thomas Cromwell coordinated the Royal Commissioners who were tasked with finding evidence of monastic corruption to enable the dissolution of the monasteries. Cromwell's spy Richard Layton wrote to him about how they proposed to obtain incriminating material to support the dissolution of the Cistercian monastery Fountains Abbey.

Fountains Abbey was seized during the dissolution of the monasteries ordered by Henry VIII and subsequently fell into disrepair. This photo of the ruins can be found in files from the Central Office of Information.

SPYDLE CHALLENGE

Reveal the innocuous-sounding name used to describe a spying excursion by which a monastery's moral validity would be judged.

To do so, solve the crossword-style clues and write the resulting words into the numbered boxes. In these boxes each letter has been replaced by a number, with each number always representing the same letter. Once you have identified which letter is represented by every number, you can complete the final row of boxes to reveal the name.

5	3	3	2	3	4	5	7	4	Aide

2	7	1	2	4	5	4	2	6	7	A request to attend

2	7	1	5	3	2	6	7	Armed infiltration

3	5	4	5	7	The Devil

3	5	2	7	4	Venerated person

Name given to the spying excursions:

1	2	3	2	4	5	4	2	6	7

Use these boxes to keep track of the code:

1	2	3	4	5	6	7

9: FABRICATED FELONIES

The *Compendium Compertorum* was a book that held evidence, obtained by Henry VIII's spies, of monastic corruption – although that evidence was very often fabricated. It indicated the kinds of 'activities' that were deemed treasonous enough to justify dissolving a monastery.

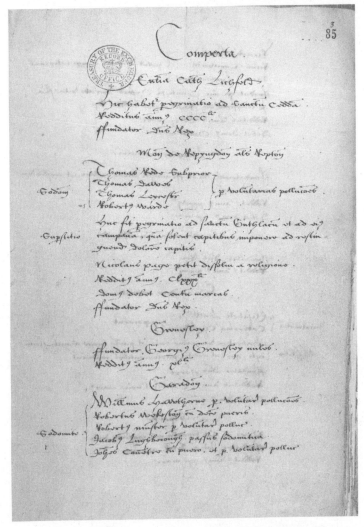

A page from the Compendium Compertorum *detailing the charges of immorality against the monks and nuns of abbeys and priories.*

SPYDLE CHALLENGE

The following religious institutions were named in the *Compendium Compertorum* along with a holy relic each was alleged to have, and a summary of their debt. Use the chart and table to work out which relic each institution possessed, and how much they owed.

- Kaldham Monalium either owed 20 marks or possessed the Tunic of St Thomas – but not both
- The Belt of St Mary was said to not be at Kaldham Monalium
- Grace Dien Monalium owes 20 pounds
- The institution with the Tunic of St Thomas owes either 20 pounds or 20 marks

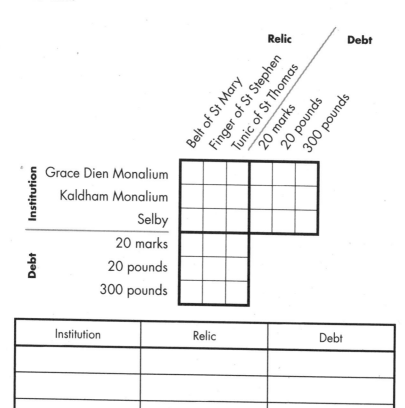

Institution	Relic	Debt

10: SPY SCHOOL

In England, the safety of Queen Elizabeth I was constantly under threat from enemies at home and abroad. Elizabeth's Secretary of State, Sir Francis Walsingham, created a school for espionage in London in the 1570s, recruiting spies and developing an unrivalled network of agents and informants throughout Europe.

Illustration of Elizabeth I in the coram rege rolls of the Court of King's Bench.

SPYDLE CHALLENGE

Imagine that you're responsible for overseeing Walsingham's spy school and need to keep track of three recruits. You want to know which location each of them was recruited from, what speciality they are trained in, and where they have been dispatched to after completing training. You also know:

- It was not the spy recruited from Cambridge University who was sent to Spain
- The spy sent to Belgium had been trained in languages
- Neither the new forger nor the decryption specialist had been recruited from London to attend the espionage school
- Decryption training was not part of the studies of the spy who had previously attended Oxford University
- One of the spies was dispatched to France

Can you now say where each spy was recruited from and where they were sent to, along with what training they received?

	Decryption	Forgery	Languages	Belgium	France	Spain
Cambridge						
London						
Oxford						
Belgium						
France						
Spain						

Trained / **Dispatched**

Recruited (rows: Cambridge, London, Oxford)
Dispatched (rows: Belgium, France, Spain)

Recruited from	Trained in	Dispatched to

11: ENEMIES OF THE CROWN

Conspiracies to overthrow Elizabeth I were uncovered by Walsingham's men throughout her reign. From 1571 to 1586, the discovery of a series of plots to establish Mary, Queen of Scots, on the throne led to the trial and execution of Mary and many of her friends and allies.

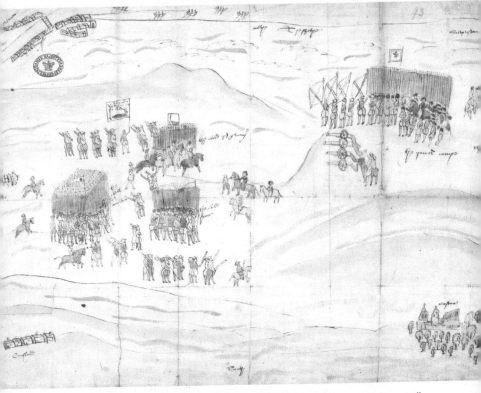

Illustration from the records of the State Papers Office of the meeting at Carberry Hill, near Edinburgh, between Mary, Queen of Scots, and the lords opposed to her, where she was double-crossed and taken prisoner on 15 June 1567.

SPYDLE CHALLENGE

Disguised below is an actual quote from one of Mary's supporters abroad, who wished to see Elizabeth removed from the throne.

Imagine that you've been recruited to intercept and decrypt messages from possible traitors. You know that the message below has been disguised with a substitution cipher, where each letter is replaced by another in the alphabet. Can you use your code-cracking skills to decipher the text and reveal the original, treasonous message?

GSVIV YV NZMB NVZMH

RM SZMW GL IVNLEV

GSV YVZHG GSZG

GILFYOVH GSV DLIOW

If you need a hint, consider that in one particular sense this message has been written 'backwards'.

A	B	C	D	E	F	G	H	I	J	K	L	M

N	O	P	Q	R	S	T	U	V	W	X	Y	Z

12: SEALED BY A SPY

Letters between Mary, Queen of Scots, and her allies in England and abroad were painstakingly deciphered and copied by Walsingham's master-forger and cipher secretary, Thomas Phelippes. Letters were then carefully resealed and sent on to their intended recipients, who blithely continued with their scheme to establish Mary on the throne.

Seals were used to indicate the legitimacy of a document. This shows the obverse of the seal that Mary, Queen of Scots, would have used to sign her letters – many of which were intercepted by Walsingham's spies.

SPYDLE CHALLENGE

Imagine that you're a spy who has received three intercepted royal letters which have each been written in code. Unfortunately, the records about each letter have become jumbled and so you now need to work out from the information you do have where each was being sent to, and in what month it was sent. You also know:

- Three letters were sent in total, each to a different country and using a different code to disguise the contents.
- The letter with the zodiac code was sent to France.
- None of the letters was sent in the same month.
- One of the letters used an alphabetical code, but it wasn't the one sent to Scotland.
- The letter sent to Spain was sent in October.
- None of the letters was sent in April, September or November.
- The letter with the number code was not the one sent in May.
- Two of the letters were sent in consecutive calendar months.

Where was each letter sent, in what month, and using which code?

Destination	Code	Month

13: DOUBLE AGENT

In 1586, Mary, Queen of Scots, was held prisoner at Chartley, a castle in Staffordshire, under the watchful eye of Sir Amias Paulet, a Protestant loyal to Elizabeth I. In Paulet's custody, Mary's contact with the outside world was limited to correspondence encrypted by her cipher secretary, Gilbert Curle, and smuggled out in casks of ale. Every letter was intercepted by a Catholic double agent, Gilbert Gifford, who had offered his services to Walsingham in 1585.

An allegorical sketch found in State Paper records of Mary, Queen of Scots, depicted here as a mermaid – a sign of prostitution – following her fall into disrepute.

SPYDLE CHALLENGE

Below is an actual quote from Gilbert Gifford, sent in a message to Sir Francis Walsingham, in which he expresses his willingness to act as a double agent – although the number encoding is for the purposes of this puzzle.

Use your codebreaking skills to decipher the original message, in which every letter in some of the crucial words has been replaced by a number.

'I have 16-10-2-36-8 of the

46-30-36-22 you do and I want

to 38-10-36-44-10 you. I have no

38-6-36-42-32-24-10-38 and no

12-10-2-36 of 8-2-28-14-10-36.

Whatever you 30-36-8-10-36 me to

do I will 2-6-6-30-26-32-24-18-38-16.'

If you need a clue, it might be worth considering why all of the numbers in the code might be even.

A	B	C	D	E	F	G	H	I	J	K	L	M
N	O	P	Q	R	S	T	U	V	W	X	Y	Z

14: MARY'S CIPHERS

Unique ciphers using specific combinations of symbols, letters, words and nulls were often used for different recipients in Tudor times to hide a letter's content from prying eyes. This document is a key to the symbols created to represent particular individuals in ciphers used by Mary, Queen of Scots, during her imprisonment at Chartley Manor.

These ciphers from Mary, Queen of Scots, were used to implicate her and bring her to trial.

SPYDLE CHALLENGE

Mary's ciphers used distinct symbols to refer to distinct individuals in her letters. The Duke of Florence, for example, was denoted with the symbol 'Σ'.

Imagine that you're one of Walsingham's spies who needs to decrypt a letter from Mary, which refers to three people each represented by a different cipher symbol. They are each a member of a different European country's royal family. The three symbols in question are shown in the table and grid below. You also know:

- The queen referred to by one of the symbols represented part of the British Isles
- The royal who was represented by the heart-shaped symbol was a prince
- The person who was replaced in the cipher by a line with two crossing lines was not a royal in the English court
- One of the symbols referred to a Scottish prince

These are the actual symbols that were used in the ciphers. Can you say which symbol was used to represent which member of which royal family?

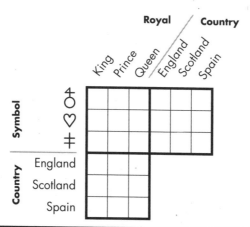

Symbol	Royal Position	Country
♂̄		
♡		
‡		

15: THE NAMES OF TRAITORS

Anthony Babington, an English gentleman and supporter of Mary, encouraged by allies, planned the assassination of Elizabeth I to install Mary on the throne. His letter, dated 6 July 1586, revealed the details of what has become known as the Babington Plot. Babington asked for Mary's approval and advice to ensure 'the dispatch of the usurping Competitor' (Elizabeth I).

Mary's reply on 17 July sealed her fate. It fell into the hands of Thomas Phelippes, who copied the letter, added the gallows sign and forged a short postscript asking Babington for the names of those involved.

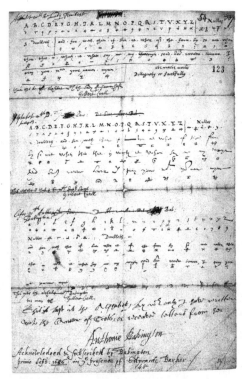

A page of ciphers found within the Tudor State Papers. The ciphers, signed by Anthony Babington in September 1586, were used as evidence in Mary's trial.

SPYDLE CHALLENGE

The names of several men involved in the Babington Plot have been given below. The names, however, have been 'intercepted', with extra letters mixed in to disguise them.

Identify the names of the men involved by removing a treasonous word from each line, to leave behind only the letters that spell out the name. There is exactly one word and one name per line.

For example, the line 'BRAEBINBGTEOLN' conceals both 'BABINGTON' and 'REBEL'. Note that all of the letters for both the name and the treasonous word remain in the correct order, and there are no letters left over.

TBRAALLIATRODR

TTICUHRBNOCRONAET

BSETALRIASBYURYER

DOSNPNY

COBANRSNPEIRWAETLOLR

PSALVOATGTEER

16: A FLEXIBLE TRAITOR

In 1571 a further plot against the Elizabethan throne was discovered, involving Philip II of Spain, Pope Pius V and the Duke of Norfolk, as well as Mary's adviser, the Bishop of Ross, and Mary herself. At its heart was Roberto Ridolfi, a Florentine banker based in London. Ridolfi travelled to Europe to raise support for an invasion of eastern England and an uprising of Catholics, which would be followed by the marriage of the Duke of Norfolk to Mary, Queen of Scots, who would seize the English throne.

An initial detail of Philip and Mary in the coram rege *rolls, dated 1558.*

SPYDLE CHALLENGE

As a banker and merchant, Ridolfi was able to move around high society in Europe without attracting too much attention.

Imagine you're questioning someone suspected of treason about their movements and alibis. They claim to have recently been to four different countries via four different means of transport, with a different motive for each of these visits. Unsurprisingly for someone suspected of treason, they're being cagey about giving out too much information. Here's what you manage to discover:

- One of the journeys was made on horseback, but it was not the one to London.
- The journey made to purchase new property was undertaken in a carriage.
- The journey to visit colleagues was made on horseback.
- The purpose of the visit to Madrid was to seek out new business.
- The journey to London was not made to collect gold.
- The spy had travelled to Brussels by boat.
- One journey was on foot, and another was to Rome.

Which four cities has the suspect been to, using which method of transport to get to each of them, and with what supposed objective in each location?

Destination	Transport	Objective

17: BEWARE EAVESDROPPERS

When Ridolfi's messenger was arrested at Dover, incriminating letters were seized and the Duke of Norfolk was arrested, tried for high treason and found guilty. He was executed on Tower Hill on 2 June 1572. Ridolfi was abroad when the plot was uncovered and so escaped this fate. Elizabeth I was, however, reluctant to authorise the execution of a fellow queen, so instead Mary, Queen of Scots, was kept under ever-tighter surveillance.

Signature of Elizabeth I, from the Tudor State Papers records.

SPYDLE CHALLENGE

Ridolfi's plot was foiled partly by his own arrogance. It's believed that his boasting about the plot was overheard by an Italian nobleman, who sent word of the conspiracy to Elizabeth I.

Can you use your own spy-tracking skills to work out which precise person it was that Ridolfi should have been more careful around? Starting on the grey square below, find a path that visits every grid square. As it travels, the path must spell out the name and title of the man who overheard the plot against the English queen. The path can only travel horizontally or vertically between squares, and will finish at the black square.

	C	D	E	M
S	O	I	D	E
I	M	O	I	C
K	U	N	A	I
E	D	D	R	G
O	U	S	N	Y
F	T	C	A	

Write out the name of the person in the area below, placing one letter per underline. The lengths of each of the various words making up the nobleman's full name are as indicated.

_ _ _ _ _ _   _   _ _   _ _ _ _ _ _,

_ _ _ _ _   _ _ _ _   _ _   _ _ _ _ _ _ _ _

18: SPIES IN SPAIN

Antony Standen was a spy who passed information from mainland Europe to Elizabeth I's 'spymaster,' Sir Francis Walsingham. His intelligence reports on the Spanish Armada made him a key figure in the Elizabethan secret service.

On one occasion, Standen borrowed 100 crowns to send an unnamed Flemish man to Lisbon. Through Standen, this spy sent vital intelligence to England about the coming Armada for the next two years. For example, he was almost certainly the source of a list of all the ships, men and supplies in the Spanish navy, which came into Walsingham's hands sometime in 1587. This information proved that the Armada would not, as England had feared, be ready to sail that year.

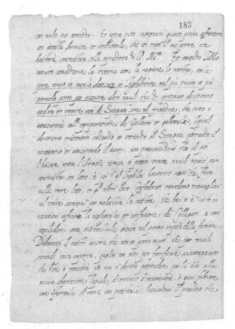

Standen's report on all the ships, men and supplies in the Spanish Armada came into Walsingham's hands sometime in 1587.

SPYDLE CHALLENGE

Imagine you've been sent a report on the Spanish Armada and are trying to establish exactly how powerful the enemy's forces are. Use the facts below to work out how many of each type of asset have been counted. Those assets are soldiers of three different nationalities, galleons and horses.

- The combined total of Spanish and German soldiers is 26,000 men
- There are ten times as many German soldiers as there are horses
- The number of Italian soldiers is three-quarters of the number of Spanish soldiers
- There are forty times as many horses as there are galleons
- There are 38,000 soldiers in total

Use the table below to record your solution:

Asset	Number
Galleons	
Spanish soldiers	
Italian soldiers	
German soldiers	
Horses	

19: ALSO KNOWN AS

Long before his key role in providing information on the Armada, spy Antony Standen had left England for Scotland in 1556 with Lord Darnley. In 1565 Standen went to France, and in the early 1580s he seems to have settled in Tuscany. He made friends with Giovanni Figliazzi, Tuscan ambassador to Madrid, and an excellent source of information about developments in Spain. Although Walsingham was probably in contact with Standen from about 1582, it was not until the spring of 1587 that a regular correspondence began and Standen started to receive £100 a year from Elizabeth I for his service as a spy.

These 'leters of Spayne' are pages from an intelligence report sent by the English spy Standen in 1587.

SPYDLE CHALLENGE

Standen used a pseudonym while he was in Florence, Tuscany. Work out what it was by solving the crossword-style clues and writing the resulting words into the numbered boxes. In these boxes each letter has been replaced by a number, with each number always representing the same letter. Once you have identified which letter is represented by every number, you can complete the final row of boxes to reveal the alias.

| 8 | 3 | 1 | 7 | 2 | 1 | 4 | 7 | Immoral; inapt |

| 4 | 9 | 6 | 8 | 9 | 4 | 4 | 7 | System designer; mechanic |

| 1 | 4 | 7 | 8 | 5 | Great danger |

| 7 | 4 | 5 | 8 | 6 | 8 | 2 | 9 | Faith system |

| 4 | 3 | 1 | 8 | 7 | 4 | Britain's was once the largest |

Antony Standen's alias:

| 1 | 2 | 3 | 1 | 4 | 2 |

| 1 | 4 | 5 | 5 | 4 | 6 | 7 | 8 | 9 | 8 |

You can use the grid below to keep track of the code:

| 1 | 2 | 3 | 4 | 5 | 6 | 7 | 8 | 9 |

20: MAKING TRACKS

Elizabeth and her travelling court's movements were surrounded in secrecy due to the fear of ambush by enemy forces. To break up journeys, the royal entourage would descend upon a trusted host's country house. Although it was an honour to receive Elizabeth, a host family's resources and supplies would be completely drained when the queen's travelling court descended upon their estate.

The image below shows the stops on a journey made by Elizabeth I in 1578. It says: 'A brief show of the situation of the several houses named in her majesty's jests with the number of miles between every of them.' The map was most likely to have been used to coordinate planning and provisions for the long journey, but it would have been dangerous for the queen if it had fallen into the wrong hands.

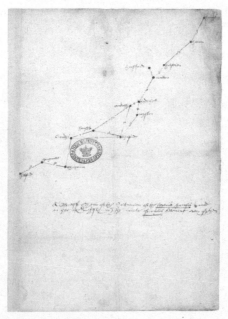

Sketch map from 1578 showing the travelling stops for Elizabeth I's court.

SPYDLE CHALLENGE

Imagine you are trying to find out the order of stopping points on a royal journey. You know that there will be seven stops on the trip, and what they are, but you don't know what order they will be in. Here's what you do know, however:

- Hatfield is the stop immediately before Harrow
- Thetford is visited before Shelford, but not immediately before
- Royston is the fourth stop on the journey
- Hampton Court is to be visited sometime after Hengrave, but not immediately after
- There is exactly one stop between Shelford and Hatfield, with Hatfield to be visited later
- Hengrave is not the first stop on the journey

Number each stop with the order in which it is to be visited (writing '1' for the first stop, '2' for the second, and so on):

Hampton Court ☐   Royston ☐

Harrow ☐   Shelford ☐

Hatfield ☐   Thetford ☐

Hengrave ☐

2 TREASON, PLOT AND REVOLUTION

The seventeenth century brought new treasons and the convulsion of civil war. The attempt by Guy Fawkes and his conspirators to blow up King James I and Parliament in the Gunpowder Plot of 1605 is perhaps the most famous act of treason of all, but it was foiled thanks to a piece of timely intelligence passed to Robert Cecil, the King's Principal Secretary, giving prior warning. With Fawkes apprehended, the search was on for his fellow conspirators, using every piece of information at the authorities' disposal.

The Gunpowder Plot was a narrow escape for the King and his government, but by 1642 England had descended into civil war – on one side, the Royalists under King Charles I, and on the other, the Parliamentarians. News was at a premium and partisan newspapers – often called 'Intelligencers' – sprang up to fill the void. They reported details such as news from the battlefield – most probably gathered from sources on active service – and even the whereabouts of the King. However, the war did not end happily for Charles I; having lost and been convicted of treason, he was executed outside the Banqueting House in Whitehall on 30 January 1649.

By the early eighteenth century, the government faced a new threat in the form of the Jacobite rebellions. King James II had been deposed in 1688; his followers, known as Jacobites, intended to restore him or his heirs to the throne. The British government therefore kept them under close surveillance and the Jacobites, in turn, conducted their own espionage on the country's defences. The reasons for this became clear in 1715 and 1745, when the Jacobites raised their own armies to take on the government. Ultimately, however, they were unsuccessful, and their movement fizzled out.

The threat of rebellion was never far away, though, and in 1789 the French Revolution reverberated across Europe. There was a fear that revolutionary ideas might find ground in Britain too, and Evan Nepean, the Under-Secretary of State for the Home Department, was kept gainfully employed hunting down subversive activity and French republicans in London's coffee houses and taverns. The need for vigilance and intelligence-gathering extended to the military campaigns being waged across Europe against Napoleon Bonaparte. The Duke of Wellington's codebreaker, George Scovell, was a master at the art of encrypting and deciphering communications and even managed to crack the French Great Cipher; this was of inestimable value in securing Wellington's victory in the Peninsular War.

21: JUICY GOSSIP

The National Archives holds hundreds of letters and documents relating to the Gunpowder Plot, a plot to blow up the entire Palace of Westminster and everyone in it. These include a sequence of letters to and from the Jesuit priest, Henry Garnet, that demonstrate a type of clandestine communication often used by the Catholic underground: 'invisible' ink.

Drawing of Henry Garnet, dated 3 May 1606, published in precis in the Calendar of State Papers Domestic, James I.

Can you detect what substance was used to create the invisible ink in many letters relating to the Gunpowder Plot?

In the list of words below, some of the letters have become 'invisible' and been replaced with an underscore. Fill in the invisible letters to create a set of related words which are all linked by a common property. Once complete, read the circled invisible letters from top to bottom to reveal the true source of the invisible ink, which also fits into the same set.

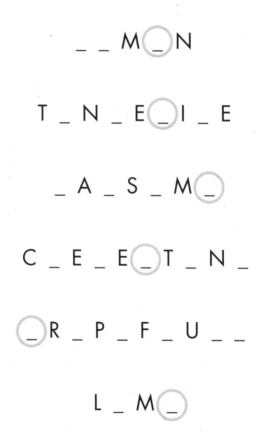

_ _ M ◯ N

T _ N _ E ◯ I _ E

_ A _ S _ M ◯

C _ E _ E ◯ T _ N _

◯ R _ P _ F _ U _ _

L _ M ◯

22: SURROUNDED BY LIES

The letter shown below contains a message written in regular ink as well as one in invisible ink, used to communicate secret plans. The 'normal' message was used as a decoy so that the letter appeared innocent to the outside world. In this case, the message referred to an object that the letter was then wrapped around and sent with.

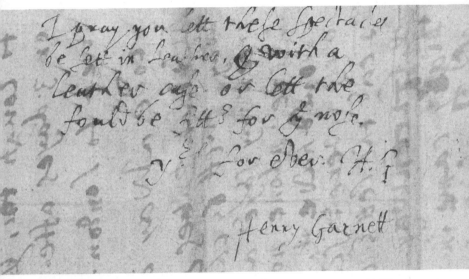

Note from Henry Garnet written with orange juice, held in records assembled by the State Paper Office.

SPYDLE CHALLENGE

Use your language and deductive skills to reveal the item around which
the letter was wrapped, the name of which can itself be found wrapped
up in the word circle below. Rearrange all of the letters to reveal the name
of the object.

Once you have identified the item, solve the following clues using the letters
found in the circle. Each solution word uses the central letter plus two or
more of the other letters, but never uses any letter more times than it appears
in the circle.

- Fortified building, such as found in Caerphilly or Edinburgh (6)
- Flee from captivity (6)
- Choose by democratic means (5)
- Formal agreement (4)
- Freedom from disturbance (5)

And then, as a further challenge, see how many more words you can form
using the same rules. As a target, try to find 35 additional words.

23: A WORD OF WARNING

The Gunpowder Plot was partly foiled by an anonymous warning sent to a Member of Parliament, warning him to stay away from the opening of Parliament on the 5 November. Halfway down the letter is written the foreboding message: *'they shall receive a terrible blow this Parliament'*.

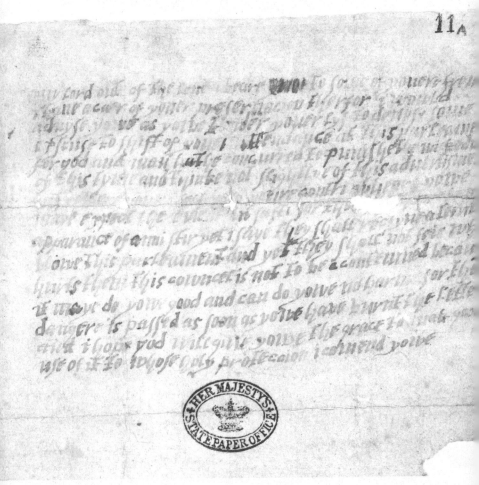

Perhaps the most famous anonymous letter in British history.

SPYDLE CHALLENGE

Reveal the name of the letter's recipient by placing one of A, E, G, L, M, N, O, R or T into each empty square, so that no letter repeats in any row, column or bold-lined 3×3 box. Once solved, the name of the Lord in question can be read down the shaded diagonal.

		G	N	A	O	L		
				T			E	
L						A		O
N					R			G
T	A						O	N
E			O					L
O		E						A
	N				O			
		M	R	G	T	O		

24: HIDDEN HERETIC

After the discovery of the Gunpowder Plot, a royal demand known as a 'proclamation' was released calling for the 'search and apprehension' of Thomas Percy. Percy had been a central figure in the plot, and was described in considerable physical detail within the proclamation:

> 'The said Percy is a tall man, with a great broad beard, a good face, the colour of his beard and head mingled with white hairs, but the head more white than the beard'.

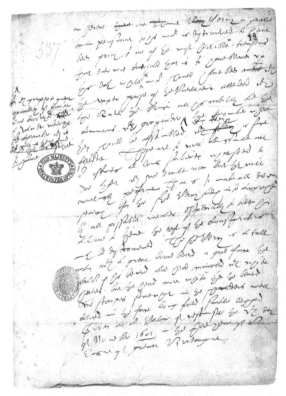

Proclamation for the arrest of the conspirator Thomas Percy, 5 November 1605.

SPYDLE CHALLENGE

Can you locate 'PERCY' within the clandestine network in which he is hiding below? Your task is to seek out the traitor's name, which can be found exactly once. To do so, start on any circle and then follow lines to touching circles, so that each circle visited in turn spells out his name. No circle can be revisited, so your path can't cross over itself or use a circle more than once. You also can't skip over any circles.

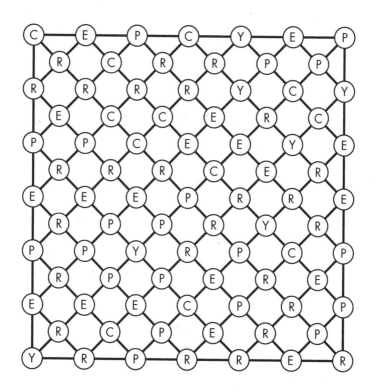

25: CONFESSION TIME

Following intelligence on his location, conspirator Thomas Percy was traced to a house in Staffordshire, in which several other plotters were also found. Thomas Wintour, one of the plotters, wrote an account of the discovery of the group; he describes his own arrival at the manor and the later arrival of the Sheriff of Worcester, whose company lay siege to the house. In the letter he writes of his co-conspirators:

> 'I asked them what they resolved to do. They answered "We mean here to die". I said again I would take such part as they did. About eleven of the clock came the company to beset the house...'

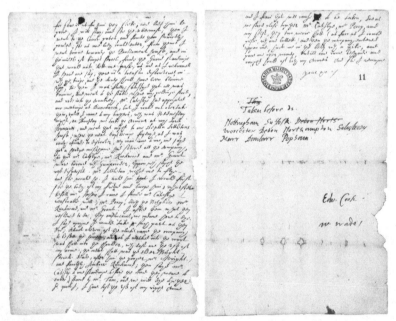

Confession of Thomas Wintour following his capture. The statement is dated 23 November 1605.

SPYDLE CHALLENGE

Work out in what order Wintour claimed each of his co-conspirators was injured by the Sheriff's men:

- Wright the Elder was injured immediately before Wright the Younger.
- Wintour was injured sometime before Rokewood, but not immediately before.
- Catesby and Percy were injured at the same time.
- Wright the Younger was not the last person to be injured.
- Rokewood was injured immediately before Catesby and Percy.

Complete the numbered list below, to show who was injured first (1) and last (5). Write the two who are described as being injured at the same time on the same row.

1. . . . .

2. . . . .

3. . . . .

4. . . . .

5. . . . .

26: THE WAR ON TRUTH

During the English Civil war, weekly newspapers sprang up to relay events to the population. Some provided foreign intelligence acquired by spies on the continent. The example pictured below is a printed 'Diurnal', as newspapers were then called, titled the *Mercurius Civicus*, or to give it its full title: '*Mercurius Civicus. Londons Intelligencer: or, Truth impartially related from thence to the whole Kingdome, to prevent mis-information*'. This was first published in May 1643 and conveyed news from the battlefield, reports from Parliament, news from London and miscellanea.

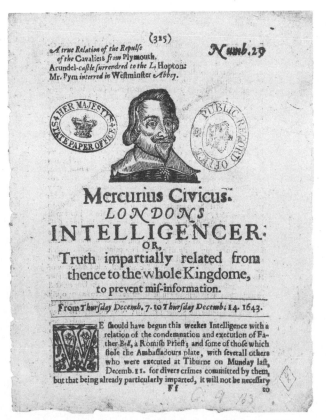

Front page of the 29th edition of the Mercurius Civicus, published in December 1643.

SPYDLE CHALLENGE

The newspaper shown opposite supported a particular group's cause during the English Civil War. Reveal the name of this group by placing A, D, E, H, N, O, R, S or U into each empty square, so that no letter repeats in any row, column or bold-lined 3×3 box. Once solved, the name of the group in question can be read down the shaded diagonal.

			D	H	N			O
		D				N	E	
	A						S	
O				E				A
U			S		O			N
S				A				E
	N						H	
	H	S				R		
A			H	S	E			

27: REBEL REPORTS

Published battlefield reports were often prefaced by the words 'the intelligence from', and it seems likely that arrangements were made with those on active service to obtain news from spies. Several pages of the *Mercurius Civicus* were set aside for reports on Royalist movements and the location of King Charles I. However, with the end of the Civil War, the *Mercurius Civicus* became redundant. It used the pages of the *Kingdomes Weekly Post* for a short while, before ceasing publication in December 1646.

The Kingdomes Weekly Post.

SPYDLE CHALLENGE

Imagine that you are editing a newspaper describing the movements of various parliamentary forces for an edition of the *Weekly Post*. There are four noblemen's forces to trace, to four different locations, and each story must be reported in a specific order.

Use the chart and table, along with your logical deduction skills, to work out where each person's forces have been traced to, and in what order the stories should be reported. You also know that:

- The House of Commons is not the place that should feature in the first report
- Chester was not the location of Sir Thomas Fairfax's forces
- The third report should be about the force in Lincolnshire
- Sir Thomas Middleton should be the subject of the first report
- Sir Thomas Fairfax's men are not at the House of Commons, nor is he the third story that should be reported
- The final report should not be about Yorkshire
- Prince de Harcourt's force was not reported to be in Lincolnshire

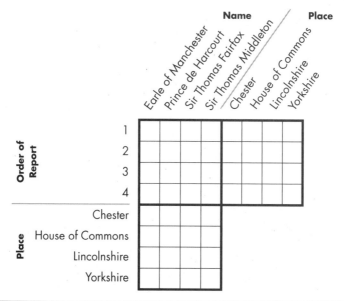

Order of Report	Name	Place
1		
2		
3		
4		

28: A SONG OF SEDITION

The Jacobites supported the restoration of the Stuart line to the thrones of England, Scotland and Ireland following the deposition of James Stuart (James II) in 1688. Jacobitism was a persistent and very real threat to the government for the best part of a century, peaking with the risings of 1715 and 1745, and so merited the attention of the government's spies. The name 'Jacobites' is taken from *Jacobus*, the Latin for James.

This 'Congratulatory hymn to his sacred Brittanick Majesty King James the III', below, is dated circa 1722. This poem was one of several vehemently Jacobite poems published in George I's reign.

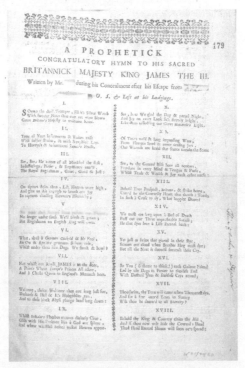

The name of the author, the place from where he escaped and the date have all been excised from this copy of the seditious song.

SPYDLE CHALLENGE

The sentence below is a particularly inflammatory one taken from the poem shown opposite. In this version of the sentence, however, the original words have been disguised in some way. Work out what change has been applied to each of the words to reveal the full, rebellious lyric.

ON EORM LHALS

NOREIGF MCUS

EOLLUTP RUO EHRONT

29: PORTSMOUTH PLANS

Throughout history intelligence obtained from spying on military defences was useful in planning offensive operations. This map was allegedly drawn by William Dunster in October 1757. He was suspected of being involved in a Jacobite spy ring, and the map was used as evidence against him.

This intriguing drawing portrays a bastion tower, complete with gun emplacements and moated outworks. It is most likely to be the fort that partially stands today to the west of Southsea Castle, in the north of Portsea Island. Its purpose was to protect the crossing at Portsbridge Creek.

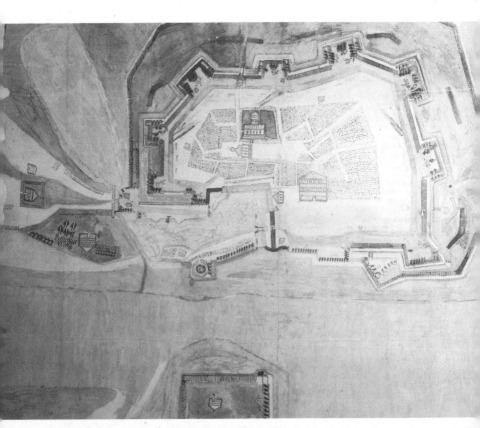

A 1757 Jacobite plan of fortifications at Portsmouth harbour.

SPYDLE CHALLENGE

Use the clues below to work out the names, professions and locations of people believed to be a part of Dunster's Jacobite spy ring. Use the chart and table, along with your logical deduction skills, to work out each alleged spy's profession and reported home location.

- Henry Page is the person at the unknown location
- Thomas Figgins is in Portsmouth
- Deptford is either the location of the tailor or of Thomas Figgins – but not both
- Mr Woodcock has an unknown profession
- The person working at the Excise Office is either the one at an unknown location or is in Fleet Street

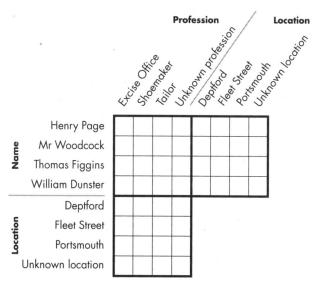

Name	Profession	Location

30: DOUBLE TROUBLE

The letter below was written by a British spy, John Roberts, who had been on a four-month fact-finding mission in the Netherlands in 1718.

In this letter, Roberts reveals the name of an informant associated with the Jacobites who had turned double agent, perhaps in an effort to save his social standing.

John Robert's letter reveals the principal informant from whom he received intelligence.

SPYDLE CHALLENGE

Reveal the name of the man believed to be a double agent by placing all of the following related words into the grid, so each reads across one row (with one letter per box). Three letters are already given. Once complete, the name of the traitor can be read down the shaded column.

Words to place:

AGENT

BRITISH

INFORMANT

INTERCEPT

JOHN

KING

LETTER

MESSAGES

MISSION

NETHERLANDS

SPY

31: A SORRY CIPHER

Ciphers were used for diplomatic correspondence as it was commonplace for them to be intercepted by host governments; more sensitive matters were written in code, usually numerical, to which only the writer and recipient had the key.

Henriette, the wife of Louis XIV's brother, Philippe, Duke of Orléans, had been sent to Dover to sign a secret treaty between France and England. She died mysteriously.

According to a report from William Perwich, an English agent in France: *'On Thursday Last Madam founde herselfe a little indisposed . . . on Sunday morning she declared she was not well without knowing what visible distemper indisposed her.'* Perwich's report then later changes into cipher.

Pamphlet of the funeral oration of Henriette
Anne d'Angleterre.

SPYDLE CHALLENGE

Use your codebreaking skills to crack the code below, in which some of the second, secret part of the original message is hidden. It's up to you, however, to work out exactly how the message has been encoded.

26 15 15   7 19 22

11 22 12 11 15 22

25 22 15 18 22 5 22

8 19 22   4 26 8

11 12 18 8 12 13 22 23

Hint: If you're stuck, try thinking about 'reversing' the cipher . . . or more specifically how would you 'reverse' the most likely meaning of the numbers?

A	B	C	D	E	F	G	H	I	J	K	L	M
N	O	P	Q	R	S	T	U	V	W	X	Y	Z

32: COFFEE CULTURE

Evan Nepean was a Napoleonic spymaster and at the young age of 29 became responsible for French naval and political intelligence in the late eighteenth century. He established a surveillance system in London by placing informers in coffee houses and taverns. His work expanded into running a network of spies across Europe. His success led to his appointment in 1794 as Under-Secretary of State for War.

Victorian depiction of Georgian coffee houses, similar to those where Nepean would have deployed his network of intelligence gatherers.

SPYDLE CHALLENGE

Imagine you are a spymaster in control of a ring of informants in central London. You have four spies in your network, each sent to a different codenamed coffee house in a different area of London, and each meeting with a foreign spy when they arrive at their designated coffee house. Use the chart, table and clues below to work out which spy has been sent where, and the nationality of the spy they are meeting.

- Soho is not the location of the coffee house codenamed Anthem
- The Turkish spy is at the place known as Duty
- The Westminster coffee house has the codename of Banner
- Neither the location codenamed King nor the one codenamed Anthem can be found in Covent Garden
- The Moroccan spy is not located at the place codenamed King
- The coffee house codenamed Banner is the location for the French spy

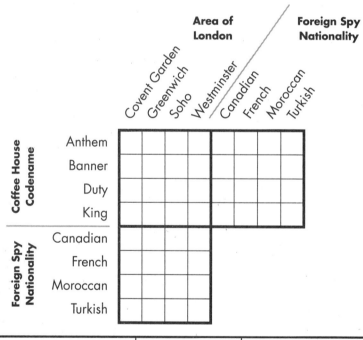

Coffee House Codename	Area of London	Foreign Spy Nationality

33: BATTLE BREAKERS

The wars that followed the French Revolution and the rise of Napoleon Bonaparte ushered in a new era of intrigue and bloodshed. Most of Europe fell before Napoleon's *Grande Armée*.

In 1808 Napoleon turned his attention to Portugal and Spain, occupying Lisbon and Madrid and placing his brother Joseph on the Spanish throne. The Portuguese and Spanish resisted and sought British aid. As a result, the first British troops set foot on Portuguese soil in the summer of 1808. For the next six years the Spanish and Portuguese fought alongside the British army and waged war on the occupying French forces. Under the command of the British military general, the Duke of Wellington, codebreaking and intelligence-gathering played an important role in British victories.

Wellington's spies were integral to the defeat of the formidable Napolean, depicted here.

SPYDLE CHALLENGE

Establish the key facts about three significant battles in which Wellington's spies and codebreakers played a part in victory. Use the chart, table and clues below to work out where and when each battle was fought, and against which leader:

- Oporto was the location of the 1809 battle
- Vittoria was either the location where Joseph Bonaparte was defeated or of the battle that took place in 1812 – but not both
- Salamanca was not where the 1813 battle took place
- 1809 was either the year of the battle in Salamanca, or the year that Soult was defeated – but not both

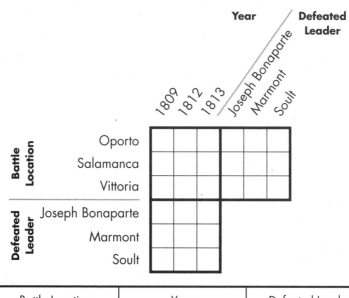

Battle Location	Year	Defeated Leader

34: THE SPY SCOVELL

George Scovell was the chief codebreaker for the Duke of
Wellington. During the Peninsular War of 1808–14 he developed
a system of military communications and intelligence-gathering
for the British, to intercept French letters and dispatches to and
from the battlefield and crack their codes. A gifted linguist, he
was placed in charge of a motley group of foreign soldiers and
deserters recruited for their local knowledge and language skills.
They became known as Scovell's Army and began to develop
a system for intercepting and deciphering encoded French
communications.

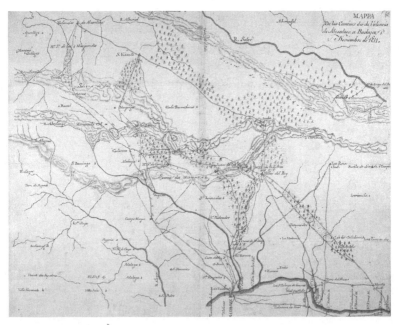

An 1811 map of Valencia and its surrounding area, from the papers of General Sir
George Scovell.

SPYDLE CHALLENGE

Use your code-cracking skills to reveal the nationalities of the soldiers commanded by Scovell, whose foreign language abilities facilitated the work of the intelligence schemes. Listed on each line below is one European nationality, although the letters in each word have been jumbled up – and some distracting spaces and punctuation added.

One additional letter has also been added per line which, when all these extra letters are extracted and read in order from top to bottom, will reveal the name given to these multilingual soldiers.

SHIP SNAG

UUPSET ROGUE

HI I, SIR!

DS IS WS

IN A LIE, TA

35: EXPLORING OFFICERS

During the Peninsular War, Wellington soon realised that the French outnumbered his forces. He therefore needed to have as much advance information as possible and so he developed a network of intelligence officers and local spies. He valued both strategic information, gathered by the interception of enemy letters, and tactical intelligence, gathered by men in the field such as 'exploring officers'.

Inspired by his military genius, many British companies used Wellington's image to portray a sense of patriotism. This image was used in a 1918 Department for National Savings advert to encourage the public to buy National War Bonds.

SPYDLE CHALLENGE

Imagine that you are overseeing the activities of three exploring officers, who are encouraged to ride behind enemy lines and gather information. Each officer has a codename and a particular skill, and each has been sent off to complete a particular reconnaissance task. Use the chart and table, along with your logical deduction skills and the clues below, to work out what skill each officer is known for, and to which task each has been assigned:

- The officer with the codename White is either a draughtsman or a linguist
- The horseman is either counting enemy troops or is codenamed Blue – but not both
- The linguist has either been tasked with intercepting letters or with counting enemy troops
- The officer codenamed Blue is a linguist

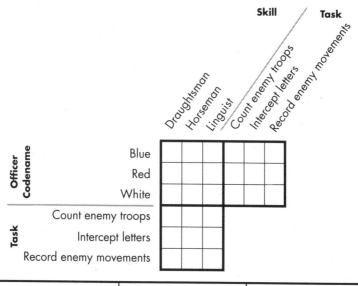

Officer Codename	Skill	Task

36: SCOVELL'S SCOPE

The French were encrypting communications using simple ciphers known as *petits chiffres*. These were designed to be written and deciphered in haste on the battlefield, and were generally short notes of instruction or orders, based initially on a system of 50 numbers. In the spring of 1811, however, they began to write letters with a more robust code based on a combination of 150 numbers. Codebreaker George Scovell cracked it within two days.

At the end of 1811, new cipher tables, known as the Great Cipher, were sent from Paris to all French military leaders. Using additional numbers, and derived from a mid-eighteenth-century diplomatic code, the tables were sent with cunning guidelines to trick the enemy, such as adding meaningless figures to the end of letters – because codebreakers would often try to tackle the end of a letter first, looking for the standard phrases that closed formal correspondence.

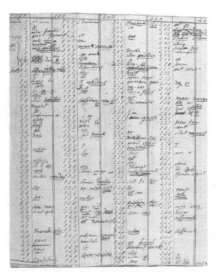

George Scovell's list of interpreted cipher words from the Great Paris Cipher (Le Grande Chiffre), 1812–13.

SPYDLE CHALLENGE

Use your numerical skills to reveal how many numbers were used in the Great Cipher, compared to the 150 of the Army of Portugal Code. To calculate this, start with the number at the top of the chain below, then follow the arrows to apply each operation in turn until you reach the 'TOTAL' box, writing your answer at the bottom. For the full Spydle challenge, try to do the entire calculation in your head without writing anything down until you reach the final TOTAL area.

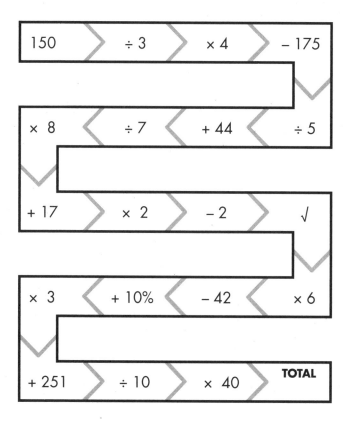

150	÷ 3	× 4	− 175
× 8	÷ 7	+ 44	÷ 5
+ 17	× 2	− 2	√
× 3	+ 10%	− 42	× 6
+ 251	÷ 10	× 40	TOTAL

How many numbers were used in the Great Cipher?

37: THE BROKEN CODE

For the next year, Scovell pored over intercepted documents.
He made gradual progress on the Great Cipher, using letters
that contained uncoded words and phrases, so that the meaning
of coded sections could be inferred from the context. The
information on troop movements gathered by Scovell's Army
Guides was also crucial when making informed guesses about the
identity of a person or place mentioned in coded letters, helping
to solve one more piece of the puzzle.

When a letter from Joseph Bonaparte to Napoleon was
intercepted in December 1812, Scovell had cracked enough of
the code to decipher most of Joseph's explicit account of French
operations and plans. This information allowed Wellington to
prepare for the final battle for control in Spain, at Vittoria, on 21
June 1813. That night, British troops seized Joseph Bonaparte's
coaches and discovered his copy of the Great Cipher – so the full
code was now revealed.

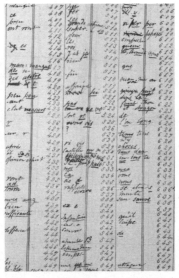

Interpreted words by Scovell.

SPYDLE CHALLENGE

Use your code-cracking skills to reveal the name of the French family of cryptographers who created the code on which the Great Cipher was based. To do so, solve the crossword-style clues below and write the resulting words into the numbered boxes. In these boxes each letter has been replaced by a number, with each number always representing the same letter. Once you have identified which letter is represented by every number, you can complete the final row of boxes to reveal the name.

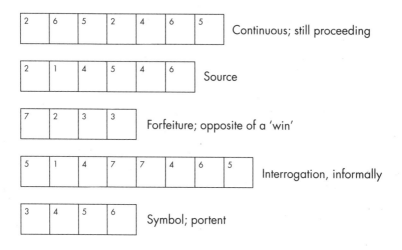

| 2 | 6 | 5 | 2 | 4 | 6 | 5 |

Continuous; still proceeding

| 2 | 1 | 4 | 5 | 4 | 6 |

Source

| 7 | 2 | 3 | 3 |

Forfeiture; opposite of a 'win'

| 5 | 1 | 4 | 7 | 7 | 4 | 6 | 5 |

Interrogation, informally

| 3 | 4 | 5 | 6 |

Symbol; portent

Name of the cryptographic family:

| 1 | 2 | 3 | 3 | 4 | 5 | 6 | 2 | 7 |

You can use the grid below to keep track of the code:

| 1 | 2 | 3 | 4 | 5 | 6 | 7 |

38: CRYPTOGRAPHY CLASSES

In 1811, George Scovell was given a book, *Cryptographia, or The Art of Decyphering* by David Arnold Conradus. It contains a series of rules and principles for creating and breaking codes and ciphers. It also provides sample problems and instructions for dealing with ciphers in English, German, Dutch, Latin, French and Italian.

Now it is well known that in English, French, German, and most languages of Western Europe, the most frequently occurring letter is *e*; the letter which follows is, in French, *n* or *s*, according to the writer; in German, *n*; in English, *t*; in Italian, *i*; and in Spanish, *a*. In Russian the most frequently occurring letter is *o*, but *i* if the language is written in Roman characters. In Polish the most frequent consonant is *z*; not uncommonly three may be found in the same word. In Arabic and Turkish the letter ‍, *elif*, corresponding to the French stopped or silent *h*, occurs oftenest. In Chinese—at least, in the newspapers—the characters found in order of frequency are 之 (*chi*, of, genitive), 不 (*puh*, not, negative), and 工 (*kong*, work). To ascertain which letters occur oftenest in any language, one must " calculate frequencies."

Cryptography continued to be a popular subject into the twentieth century. Above is an extract from André Langie's Cryptography, *published in 1922.*

SPYDLE CHALLENGE

Imagine you have discovered a book on cryptography which gives examples of types of code in different languages, and suggests points of weakness for when you begin cracking a new code. Use the following clues, along with the chart, to complete the table below.

- Latin is not the language used for the transposition example
- The index code type is shown being used with a point of weakness based either on short words or on vowels
- Similarly, Dutch is used to demonstrate a point of weakness based either on short words or on vowels
- The index code type does not use Latin
- The vowel weakness is demonstrated with a substitution code

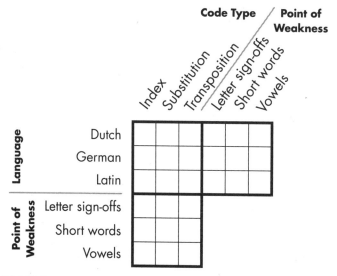

Language	Code Type	Point of Weakness

39: INDEXICAL INTELLIGENCE

Scovell experimented with different encryption methods based on the principles outlined in *Cryptographia*. He devised a method to ensure that the British had a common cipher to protect their dispatches by sending copies of the same book to each headquarters. Using his system, '56C2' would direct the reader to page 56, column C and the second word down. Although simple, this was a strong and successful code.

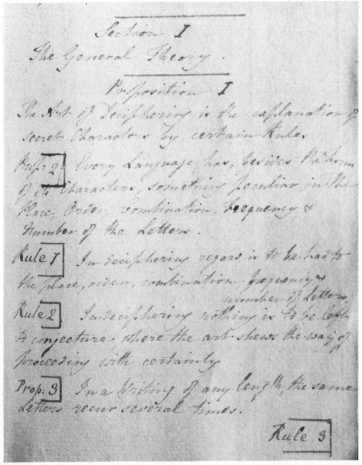

The art of deciphering: the rules of Scovell's 'The General Theory'.

SPYDLE CHALLENGE

Use your language skills to reveal the type of book sent to each headquarters for use in Scovell's code. Form the ten-letter word by starting on any letter in the grid below and then tracing a path that spells out the word by moving only to touching squares, including diagonally touching squares, and without revisiting any square. What kind of book was the key to cracking the code?

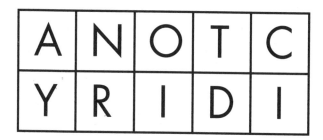

Once you've found the clued word, see how many other, shorter words you can find using the same restrictions. Each word must be at least three letters in length, and proper nouns do not count. There are at least 20 words to be found.

40: GRIDS AND GRAPHEMES

This document shows one of the many simple ciphers that George Scovell solved. Once he had passed the deciphered versions of letters to the Duke of Wellington, he was seemingly allowed to keep many of the original encrypted letters, which have survived together with his calculations. They can be seen in his papers held at The National Archives.

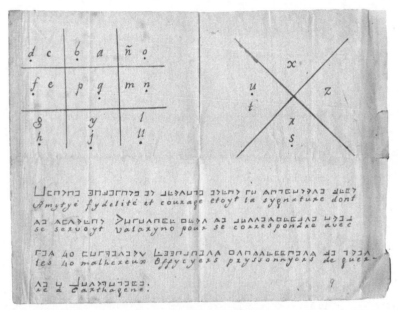

Cipher from General George Scovell's papers, 1808–14.

SPYDLE CHALLENGE

The cipher shown opposite closely resembles a modern substitution cipher known as Pigpen, which uses a system of simple symbols to replace letters. The symbols are based on the alphabetical position of letters within square and diagonal grids, which provide a key to crack the code.

Use your sleuthing skills to decipher the following words which have been encoded in Pigpen, to reveal a type of warfare used in the Peninsular War. To do so, solve the clues and then progressively crack the symbol code, in which each letter has been replaced by a symbol. Each symbol always represents the same letter, and vice versa.

Estimate or determine an amount

Against the law

Region

Someone who does not tell the truth

Inconsistent; not following the rules

Type of warfare used in the Peninsular War:

You can use the grid below to keep track of your working out:

41: AN OFFICER AND A GENTLEMAN

Lt Colonel Colquhoun Grant was one of Wellington's most trusted and experienced officers, with a reputation for being intelligent and fearless. He prided himself on always wearing his uniform, even behind enemy lines so as not to be considered a spy.

On 16 April 1812, Grant and his local guide found themselves surrounded by French soldiers near the Spanish-Portuguese border. His linguistic skills and gentlemanly behaviour earned him the respect of the French, and he even dined with one of Napoleon's top marshals.

Early nineteenth-century engraved map of Spain and Portugal.

SPYDLE CHALLENGE

Imagine you have been placed in charge of questioning a recently captured enemy officer and finding out where they claim to have been prior to being caught. They have told you the following:

- Lisbon was visited at some point between Bailen and Valencia, although not necessarily in that order
- Madrid was visited later than Valencia, but not immediately after
- After leaving Cadiz, the officer went directly to Albuera
- Lisbon was visited after – but not immediately after – Cadiz
- Corunna appeared on their itinerary somewhere between Cadiz and Lisbon, although not necessarily in that order
- Cadiz was visited immediately after Madrid
- At some point they also visited Talavera

In what order did they visit each of the locations prior to their capture? Number each location with the order in which it was visited (writing '1' for the first location, '2' for the second, and so on):

Albuera ☐   Lisbon ☐

Bailen ☐   Madrid ☐

Cadiz ☐   Talavera ☐

Corunna ☐   Valencia ☐

42: RANK FOR RANK

In the nineteenth century, spying was still considered an underhand and dishonest way of warfare. To brand Colquhoun Grant a spy would have been to cast doubt on his status as an officer and a gentleman.

While the French held Grant captive, Wellington received word that Marshal Marmont, Napoleon's aide-de-camp, was willing to make an exchange of prisoners. He did not, however, believe the French offer, because of a letter that had been intercepted by Spanish guerrillas. The letter and an attached parole document were written *en clair*, i.e., in plain script, rather than code or cipher.

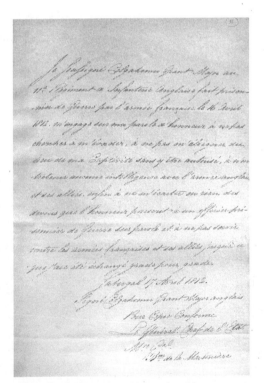

Copy of Colquhoun Grant's signed parole,
28 April 1812.

SPYDLE CHALLENGE

The text below is a transcription of parole papers signed by Grant, who agreed not to pass on any intelligence, or fight against Napoleon's forces, until he was no longer a prisoner of war. According to a common practice, he should be swapped 'rank for rank' with an equivalent prisoner of war from the French forces.

Several pairs of crucial words in this version of the transcript, however, have been swapped 'rank for rank' – which in this case means that swapped pairs of words have the same number of letters in each word. For example, 'RANK' and 'FILE' could be swapped with one another because they are the same length, but 'WAR' and 'PAROLE' could not.

Can you reveal the entirety of the transcription by un-swapping the pairs? There are six pairs in total, each of a different 'rank'.

I, the undersigned, Colquhoun Grant, April in the 11th Regiment of the English infantry, taken prisoner of war by the parole army on the 16th of Major 1812, undertake on my French of honour not to pass to escape or to remove myself from the place of my exchanged without permission, and not to seek any intelligence to the perform army and its allies; in fact, not to depart in any way from the duties which an officer Portugal of war on parole is honour bound to English; and not to serve against the French army and its allies until I have been captivity, rank for rank.

Prisoner 17 April 1812.

FIRST WORLD WAR

Spying becomes more prevalent during times of conflict, as nations seek an advantage on the battlefield, and the First World War was no exception. This was when modern signals intelligence came of age; Britain's modern-day Government Communications Headquarters (GCHQ) has its roots in 'Room 40', the naval cryptanalysis section formed in October 1914. It was Room 40 that intercepted the infamous Zimmermann telegram from the eponymous German Foreign Minister to the Mexican government. Its explosive contents – an alliance between Germany and Mexico that would reward the latter with its lost territories – had dramatic consequences, for when its existence was publicised in the USA, the American public was outraged. This helped to swing the pendulum of public opinion more decisively in favour of US entry into the war. On 6 April 1917, the USA declared war on Germany.

While the technology to transmit and intercept messages may have advanced, many aspects of spying remained recognisable from earlier eras. Codes were still used – something that George Scovell would have been familiar with during the Peninsular Wars a century before. Espionage relied heavily on the individual recruited to infiltrate another country and furtively pass secrets back, often using ingenious methods to cover their tracks. One of these methods was invisible ink, unchanged – incredibly – from the days of the Gunpowder Plot.

A huge advance in espionage during the First World War was the use of aerial reconnaissance through powered flight, although spying on the enemy from the air was, in fact, nothing new. Hot-air balloons had been used for this purpose as far back as 1794, but the invention of the first powered aeroplane and its successful flight by the Wright brothers in 1903 changed everything. The newly formed Royal Flying Corps, the air arm of the British army in the First World War, could photograph sites of interest with its aircraft. These included the German trenches on the Western Front and, in 1915, the Gallipoli peninsula in preparation for an Allied assault on Germany's ally, the Ottoman Empire.

The spies of the First World War tried hard to conceal their activities, but they were not always successful. Documents at the National Archives are full of cases of individuals who had been caught spying for Germany and faced prison or execution – none more famous than Mata Hari, the exotic dancer who was convicted of espionage by France in 1917. The Tower of London would once again be used as a place of execution, this time for spies; eleven met this fate here during the First World War.

43: KIEL CANAL

The Kiel Canal in Germany connects the Baltic Sea to the North Sea, so that vessels do not have to sail around Denmark. It was completed in 1895 and opened by Kaiser Wilhelm II, but subsequently had to be widened to accommodate Germany's new fleet of dreadnought battleships. The work of widening the canal took place between 1907 and 1914.

Britain conducted espionage on the canal because its expansion would make it easier for Germany's dreadnoughts to challenge the might of the Royal Navy.

A 1918 map of Kiel harbour and canal.

SPYDLE CHALLENGE

The map opposite is labelled with several 'vulnerable points', with additional detail on what exactly can be found at each of the numbered points. The labels for some of those extra details are given below. Fit all of the given words into the grid, so they read either across or down, with one letter per box. Ignore any spaces. Once all of the words have been entered, the letters in the shaded squares can be rearranged to reveal a type of vessel thought to have been constructed in the area shown.

5-letter word	8-letter words	9-letter words	10-letter words
LOCKS	BARRACKS	AERODROME	AIR STATION
	FORTRESS	ANCHORAGE	POWER PLANT
6-letter words	WORKSHOP	NAVAL YARD	
BRIDGE		YACHT CLUB	11-letter words
STORES			BOILER HOUSE
			ROYAL PALACE

44: A NEW DIVISION

The Naval Intelligence Department (NID) was formed in 1886 and provided much of the First World War and pre-First World War codebreaking expertise. It concerned itself with all aspects of enemy and allied shipping. It reported on intelligence such as foreign naval strength and coastal defences.

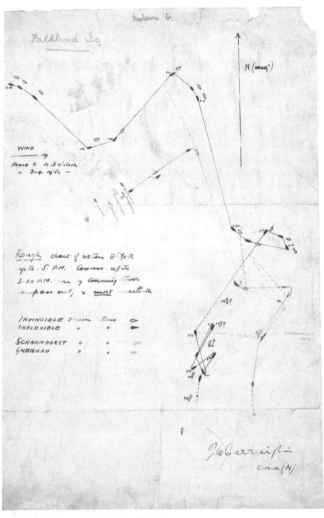

A 1914 track chart of HMS Inflexible.

SPYDLE CHALLENGE

Use your linguistic skills to work out which government department the NID was a part of. Jumbled up in the porthole below are the letters of the one-word government department, which can be formed using each letter exactly once.

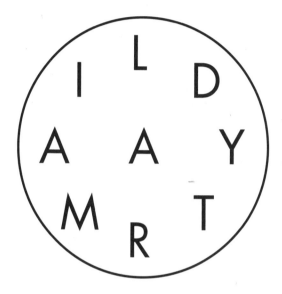

How many additional words can you form that use the centre letter plus two or more of the other letters? No letter may be used more times than it appears within the circle. There are over 60 additional words to find, and proper nouns are not accepted.

45: DETERMINED DEFENCE

The Naval Intelligence Department plotted shipping movements, specifically of enemy surface cruisers and submarines. It collected information on the topography of foreign countries, particularly coasts, and on coastal defences.

PLAN SHOWING TRACKS OF TORPEDOES.

Line drawing of HMS Britannia with U-boat periscope and torpedo tracks, from First World War Admiralty records.

SPYDLE CHALLENGE

Imagine you have been given the following reports on an enemy island's assets, and need to establish exactly what defences are on each section of coastline, along with the terrain which surrounds it. Use your deductive skills to complete an intelligence report based on the partial information presented to you. Use the following information, along with the cross-reference chart, to complete the report table below:

- The submarine nets are either near grassland or tree-covered terrain
- The tree-covered terrain is not to the north
- The sandy shore is not in the south
- The grassland is either to the west or is defended with barracks, but not both
- The barracks are not to the north, and nor is the rocky coastline near them
- The tree-covered coastline is either where the battery is or to the north, but not both

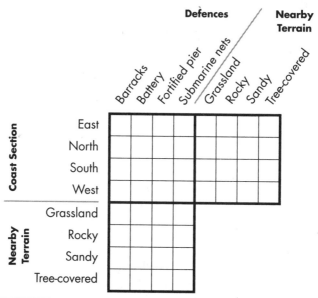

Coast Section	Defences	Nearby Terrain

46: HIDING IN PLAIN SIGHT

Part of the initial role of the Naval Intelligence Department was to plot the trajectory and position of enemy vessels, with the aim of informing strategic planning for possible warfare.

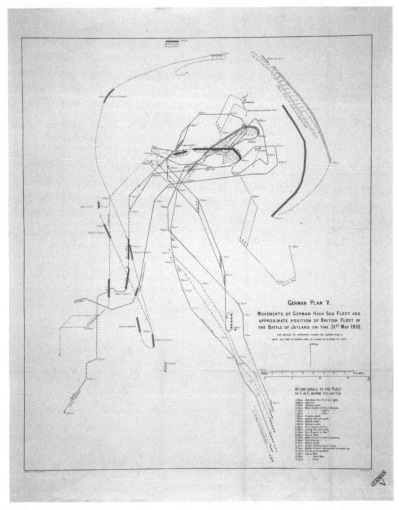

'German Plan V' – Map of German and British fleets during the Battle of Jutland, 1916.

SPYDLE CHALLENGE

Imagine you have been tasked with writing a report on the positions of various enemy ships. You know which ships are in the area and have just received some coded intelligence to help you work out exactly where each vessel is.

Place the given set of 11 ship segments into the grid, so that no completed ships touch one another – not even diagonally. Clues outside the grid reveal the number of squares containing ship segments in each row and column. Some ship parts are already given in the grid.

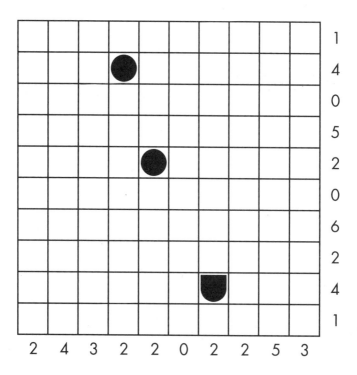

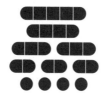

47: LUCKY ACQUISITIONS

The deciphering section of the Naval Intelligence Division, formed in October 1914, was known as 'Room 40'.

Some of Room 40's early decoding successes were owed to the chance discovery of enemy codebooks, which revealed the means to decipher messages which would otherwise have been impenetrable. One of the codebooks was found on board a run-aground ship off the coast of Estonia.

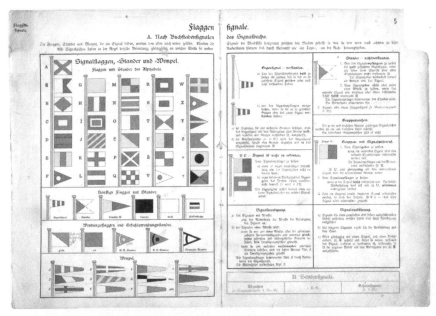

Pages on flag signals from a codebook captured from a German cruiser by Russians and handed to Room 40.

SPYDLE CHALLENGE

Reveal the name of the ship by placing one each of the letters A, B, D, E, G, M, R, S and U into each empty square, so that no letter repeats in any row, column or bold-lined 3×3 box. Once solved, the name of the ship can be read down the shaded diagonal.

					S		G	
U		D				E		
S				A			U	
		B		U				A
	D		R		G		M	
E				S		G		
	S			R				B
		A					M	E
	U		B					

48: SHARING IS CARING

Three codebooks in particular were the key to Room 40's early success, and each of these was acquired under distinct circumstances. Each codebook was found on a boat, but all three boats had been seized in different areas, and each book discovered by a different group.

The German navy's SKM code, short for Signalbuch der Kaiserlichen Marine, was found in this codebook governing German naval and diplomatic communications.

SPYDLE CHALLENGE

Use your deductive skills to establish where each codebook was found, and by whom. To do so, use the chart and table along with the following information:

- The Verkehrsbuch (VB) was either found by the British trawler or the Royal Navy
- The Russian forces did not find anything near Australia, and nor was that where the Verkehrsbuch (VB) was found
- The Netherlands was the location where either the British trawler or the Royal Navy recovered a codebook
- Either the Royal Navy found a codebook off the coast of Australia, or they retrieved the Signalbuch der Kaiserlichen Marine (SKM) – but not both

		Coastal Area Found			Found by Whom		
		Australia	Estonia	Netherlands	British trawler	Royal Navy	Russian forces
Name of Book	Handelsverkehrsbuch (HVB)						
	Signalbuch der Kaiserlichen Marine (SKM)						
	Verkehrsbuch (VB)						
Found by Whom	British trawler						
	Royal Navy						
	Russian forces						

Name of Book	Coastal Area Found	Found by Whom

49: AREAS OF INTEREST

While the three codebooks found on foreign ships were helpful in establishing Room 40's early successes in deciphering, they were not the only codes used by German intelligence during the war. Indeed, the codes from the three captured books were eventually replaced in the coming years – but there was a clear need for a dedicated team to intercept and decipher enemy signals.

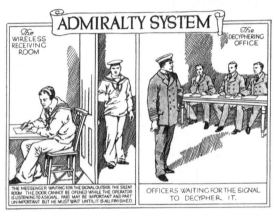

Page from a 1914 report on Rear Admiral Sir Percy Scott's cypher machine for faster signalling.

SPYDLE CHALLENGE

Imagine that you have managed to crack an enemy code, and revealed the names of several sea areas in which the enemy's naval forces are planning upcoming attacks. You need to establish the order in which the attacks are anticipated to take place, so that you can mobilise accordingly.

- Fisher will be attacked before Humber
- Wight is before but not immediately before Forties
- Dogger will be the first to be attacked
- Tyne will come before Fisher, with just one attack in-between them
- After Wight there will be one more attack before Tyne
- Fisher is before but not immediately before Thames

Number each sea area with the order in which the attacks are planned:

Dogger ☐   Humber ☐

Fisher ☐   Thames ☐

Forth ☐   Tyne ☐

Forties ☐   Wight ☐

50: NO SIGNS OF REMORSE

The image shown below gives several examples of wireless signals used by German forces, with their equivalent meanings on the right. Additionally, there are some Morse code signals shown at the bottom of the page, under the heading Special Signals.

German wireless signals listed in a 1914 Naval Intelligence Division logbook. A note on the document indicates 'these [signals] vary from time to time'.

SPYDLE CHALLENGE

Use your code-cracking skills to decipher the names of these six British coastal towns, which have been given in Morse code. You have *not* been given a guide to decoding Morse, however, so you must use the county clues alongside your own geographical knowledge to determine what each location is. Repeating letters are a good place to start.

-... --- ..- .-. -. . -- --- ..- - ....

Dorset

..-. -.. .-. -- --- ..- - ....

Cornwall

.-.. --- .-. - ... -- --- ..- - ....

Hampshire

... --- ..- - .... .-.. --- .-. -

Merseyside

- .-.. -. . -- --- ..- - ....

Tyne and Wear

.-- . .-. -- --- ..- - ....

Dorset

51: TRAFFIC ANALYSIS

Signals intelligence (SIGINT) is a method of gathering intelligence by intercepting communications. It played a huge role in the turnaround of intelligence services in the early twentieth century. Even when individual codes could not be intercepted or broken, it was possible for Room 40 to locate the source of a particular signal, and therefore establish where the target of an upcoming attack might be.

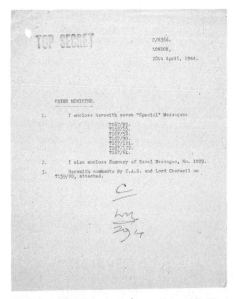

Signals intelligence passed on to Prime Minister Winston Churchill, April 1944.

SPYDLE CHALLENGE

Imagine you're in charge of deducing the origin of enemy signals and using them to work out their likely plan of attack. There are four signal sources, four potential targets, and an order in which they are likely to occur. The sources and targets are all naval vessels and have all been given codenames.

Use the following clues, along with the chart and grid, to work out which sources are linked to which targets, and in which order the attacks are likely to occur:

- Snake is not the source of the third attack
- Either the source for the second attack is Scorpion, or Star is the likely target of it – but not both
- Breeze is not the likely target from the source codenamed Scorpion
- Snake did not reveal the attack aimed at Star
- The first attack is to be on Willow
- The attack on Cormorant was sourced from Hammer

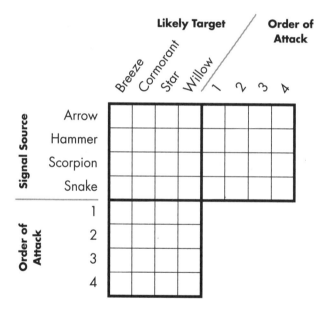

Signal Source	Likely Target	Order of Attack
		1
		2
		3
		4

52: FOILED BY FOLIAGE

The Gallipoli campaign was a First World War campaign by
Britain, France and Russia to inflict a strategic defeat on the
Ottoman Empire, which was allied to Germany as part of the
Central Powers. The plan was for British, Australian, New
Zealand and French forces to land on the Gallipoli peninsula in
Turkey, relieving pressure on the Russians in the Caucuses and
theoretically diverting Central Power resources from the Western
Front. Air reconnaissance and intelligence gathering were carried
out to discover assets and potential threats on the ground in the
Gallipoli peninsula.

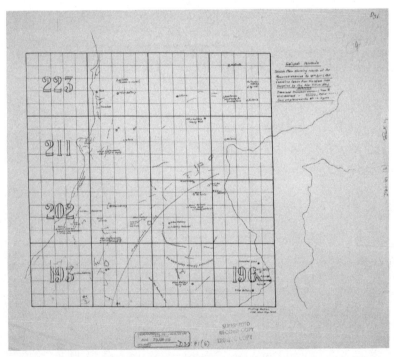

*Sketch plan showing results of air reconnaissance to 18 April 1915 in the Gallipoli
peninsula. The coastline is traced from a map supplied by the War Office.*

SPYDLE CHALLENGE

The image opposite gives details of several defences on the ground in the Gallipoli peninsula. At the bottom tip of the map, an area of forest is described as 'thoroughly reconnoitred', although it acknowledges that concealment of weapons or defences would be easy.

Use your code-cracking and observation skills to reveal a hidden item in each of the six lines below. Each item is a feature or object which has been labelled on the map opposite, but in the text below it has been 'concealed' by a tree. More specifically, the names of trees have been mixed with the names of the items, with one item and one tree per line. All the letters remain in the correct order for each word.

CAMASPH

WTIRLELNOCWH

BEPEIECRH

CHOHEWSTINTUZETR

CSYTPRERAEMSS

OROAKAD

53: COUNTING CAMPSITES

The map below was compiled from aerial reconnaissance in
April 1915, showing another part of the Gallipoli peninsula. The
positions of several gun batteries are given, and encampments and
other geographical features are marked on the map.

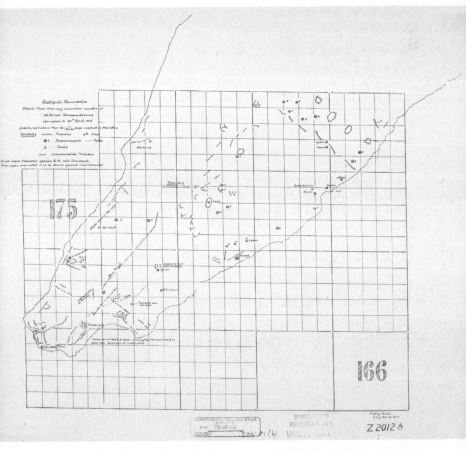

*Sketch plan of the Gallipoli peninsula showing amended results of aerial
reconnaissance to 20 April 1915.*

SPYDLE CHALLENGE

Use your deductive skills to establish the numbers of tents and guns in certain grid squares on the map, from partial information. Based on the clues and the chart, fill out the table to show how many tents and guns are located in each grid square.

- Grid square 224 is the place with 8 guns
- There are no tents at the site with 25 guns
- The place with 14 guns is not the location with 15 tents
- The 20 tents are accompanied by 8 guns
- 25 guns are either at grid square 196 or the site with 732 tents – but not both
- Grid square 202 is either the place with 28 guns or with 20 tents – but not both

	No. of Tents				No. of Guns			
	0	15	20	732	14	25	28	8
196								
202								
203								
224								
14								
25								
28								
8								

Grid Square Reference (left) / No. of Guns (lower left)

Grid Square Reference	No. of Tents	No. of Guns

54: DIRE STRAITS

The Gallipoli campaign was unsuccessful for the Allied forces, who were ultimately defeated and had to evacuate the Gallipoli peninsula in December 1915. In particular, there were several routes to the Black Sea which remained closed to the Allies; one of the original aims of the campaign had been to secure access for Allied supplies to Russia. One of these passages was the Dardanelles, which is shown in the map below.

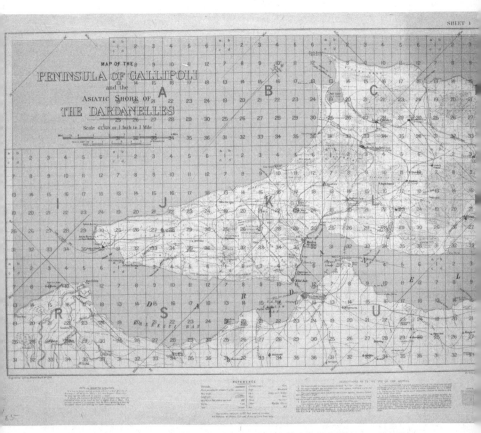

War Office map of the Gallipoli peninsula and the Asiatic shore of the Dardanelles.

SPYDLE CHALLENGE

Use your logic and code-cracking skills to reveal the name of another strategic strait which remained closed off to the Allied forces. Place B, D, H, O, P, R, S, T or U into each empty square, so that no letter repeats in any row, column or bold-lined 3x3 box. Once solved, the name of the strait can be read down the shaded diagonal.

		R	T				S	
T		D						
			O		B		H	T
		H		D		S		B
			S		R			
S		P		B		H		
P	S		B		U			
						P		O
	D				H	B		

55: SUBTLE SUBTERFUGE

The Zimmermann telegram was a secret communication on
16 January 1917 between the German Foreign Minister, Arthur
Zimmermann, and the Mexican government. It indicated that
unrestricted submarine warfare by Germany was likely to bring
the US into the First World War on the side of the Allies, and
asked if Mexico would join the war on Germany's side.

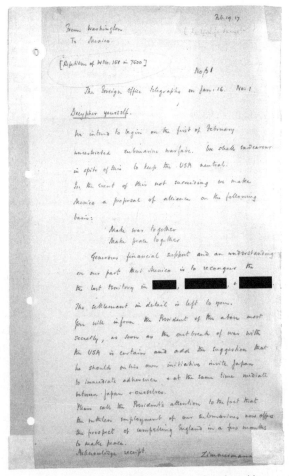

*Transcription of the Zimmermann message deciphered by
British cryptographer Nigel de Grey in January 1917.*

SPYDLE CHALLENGE

Imagine you are in charge of detecting enemy submarines and charting their current positions in anticipation of imminent attack. The data you have is based on sonar readings, and it's up to you to use it to plot the exact locations of hidden submarines on a map of a particular sea area.

The numbers in some squares reveal the total number of submarines in touching squares – including diagonally. You know that submarines can't be located in the numbered squares, however, and that there is no more than one submarine per square. Can you locate them all? How many submarines are hiding in this sea area?

	2		2	1			1
2	4	2			3	1	
	2		4		2		1
2	3	3		3		1	
					1		2
3	4		3				
		3		2	3	2	
	4		2		2		1

56: TERRITORIAL TEMPTATIONS

With the British having cut their telegraphic cables in the English Channel, the Germans had to find alternative ways to send telegrams to their North American diplomatic missions. This included the 'Swedish roundabout' method where coded telegrams were sent via the Swedish Foreign Ministry, disguised as Swedish diplomatic messages. In a wish to bring peace to Europe, President Wilson also allowed the Germans to send telegrams through US diplomatic channels, and Zimmermann used this channel to send Germany's offer to Mexico.

In an effort to persuade Mexico to join with them, Zimmermann suggested that Mexico would be allowed to regain territory previously lost to the US, if Germany was victorious.

In particular, the Zimmerman telegram listed three US states that Mexico could expand into in the event of a successful campaign.

Example of an intercepted 'Swedish roundabout' telegram sent by Zimmermann, disguised as a message from the Swedish government.

SPYDLE CHALLENGE

Use your observation skills to reveal the names of the three US states mentioned in the Zimmermann telegram, by working out which three of the 38 states listed below cannot be found in the word search grid. The other states can be found in straight lines, and may be written in any direction, including diagonally or backwards. Which three states are missing?

ALABAMA	INDIANA	MONTANA	SOUTH DAKOTA
ALASKA	IOWA	NEBRASKA	TENNESSEE
ARIZONA	KANSAS	NEVADA	TEXAS
CALIFORNIA	KENTUCKY	NEW MEXICO	UTAH
COLORADO	LOUISIANA	NEW YORK	VERMONT
DELAWARE	MAINE	NORTH CAROLINA	VIRGINIA
FLORIDA	MARYLAND	OHIO	WISCONSIN
GEORGIA	MICHIGAN	OKLAHOMA	WYOMING
HAWAII	MINNESOTA	OREGON	
IDAHO	MISSOURI	PENNSYLVANIA	

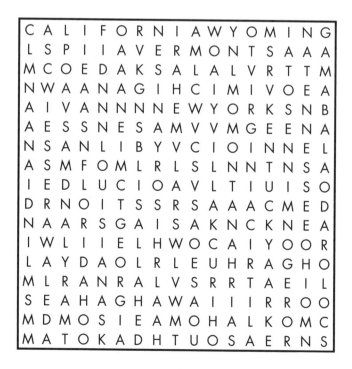

57: FOR YOUR EYES ONLY

Deciphering the Zimmerman telegram was a turning point in the war, as its discovery would be instrumental in persuading the United States of America to enter the First World War, but Room 40 was still faced with a delicate diplomatic situation. In informing the US of the telegram's contents, they would also have to admit that they were intercepting communications sent through Washington, which the telegram had been.

SECRET.

L.W.   February 24th 1 p.m. 1917.

Balfour has handed me the translation of a cipher message from Zimmermann, the German Secretary of State for Foreign Affairs, to the German Minister in Mexico, which was sent via Washington and relayed by Bernstorff on January 19th.

You can probably obtain a copy of the text relayed by Bernstorff from the cable office in Washington. The first group is the number of the telegram, 130, and the second is 13042, indicating the number of the code used. The last but two is 97556, which is Zimmermann's signature.

Note of US Ambassador Walter Page's telegram to the US Secretary of State, including the English translation of Zimmermann's message, 24 February 1917.

SPYDLE CHALLENGE

Imagine you are responsible for justifying how the document came into your possession, and need to come up with a set of potential explanations for how you gained access to a sensitive telegram sent between Germany and Mexico. You have narrowed it down to three options, and three ways you might communicate the news to the US.

Use the chart, grid and the clues below to work out the options being considered, and their current order of preference.

- Your third preference is not the option of claiming that the document leaked in Germany
- A telephone call is your most-preferred notification option
- Saying that the document leaked in Germany is not your most-preferred option
- Claiming that the document leaked in Mexico is not your third preference
- Notifying via a letter is not your second preference

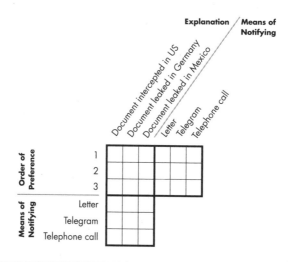

Order of Preference	Explanation	Means of Notifying
1		
2		
3		

58: THE SOUND OF A SPY

Kurt Herlot de Rysbach, a British subject and son of a naturalised Austrian, was arrested on 26 July 1915 as an enemy spy. He was subsequently convicted at the Central Criminal Court for attempting to communicate information regarding HM Forces with the intention of assisting Germany in the First World War, for which he was sentenced to penal servitude for life.

Courtenay de Rysbach in German military uniform.

Newspaper clipping of German spy Kurt de Rysbach found in Home Office files.

SPYDLE CHALLENGE

Use your code-cracking skills to reveal five potential codenames concealed by what appears to be musical notation below. You will not need any musical knowledge to crack this code.

All you need to know is that the following set of notes represents 'AIDE':

Given this, what names do each of the following sets of notes reveal? As a clue, one of the names suggests they are the most important of the group.

59: MUSICAL MASK

Kurt Herlot de Rysbach, the enemy spy, didn't use musical notation as a code, unlike in the puzzle on the previous page, but he *did* use sheet music. Instead of changing the notes, however, he wrote secret messages to his handlers by using lemon juice as an invisible ink.

Invisible ink message written on a music sheet by German spy Kurt Herlot de Rysbach, dated 1914–15, and used in the criminal prosecution against him.

SPYDLE CHALLENGE

Imagine you have been tasked with deciphering the correspondence of a spy who has been sending secret notes via sheet music. You have received four different pieces of music, each by a different composer, which contain four pieces of information. Each piece of music was sent to a different city. Use the chart, table and clues below to work out where each piece of music was sent, with what message, and hidden on the music of which composer:

- The sheet music sent to Hamburg is either by Beethoven or is about a general strike being launched – but not both
- The financial accounts are encoded in a Strauss piece
- The Mozart sheet music for Berlin does not reveal information about the location of a factory
- The information about troop movements was encoded into either a Beethoven or a Strauss piece
- Strauss's music was sent to Munich

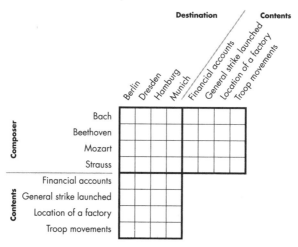

Composer	Destination	Contents

60: A CALL TO ARMS

The transcriptions of enemy spy Kurt Herlot de Rysbach's secret messages reveal that he passed a wide variety of information on to his handlers.

C.(Continued).
Page 2.

Page 3:

You will no doubt be very surprised to hear from me after such a long time. Well the Police have been giving me a very busy time just lately. It seems someone knew I had been a prisoner over here. I think it must have been a woman as I met two or three I used to know in Berlin well. A man in Ruheleben has written and told her I was naturalised and was fighting at the front with the Germans of course. I have had to do a lot of explaining lately and everything was searched but nothing found, and to-day I have decided to send you some news again. I don't think I am watched any more now. First of all there is a great scare over here now, every one is talking about conscription. This is sure to come and I must before long get out of this before it is too late. Then all the Belgian officers and men have been recalled to the front who came on holidays here. I spoke to some officers Belge 4 days ago and movement is being prepared and that this is to come off in a fort-night's time. Yesterday COOO artillery troops left for the Dardanelles. I could not send wire in code as I have no code word for Dardanelles. Saturday night there is a removal (of) 3000 Infantry and Army Service Corps (Trans-port) are leaving Southampton for Calais and from Plymouth 4200. One Battalion of Engineers sappers, etc., and 4th Battalion Welsh Fusiliers are to leave and proceed to Etampes near Calais.

Page 4:

If you could only send me some money I could get my brother who is in the Navy to give me all the Navy move-ments. He could be most valuable but he would want money for it. I expect in two weeks to be an interpreter at least I have good hopes and then can give you much more information. Like I am doing now is very difficult. The people know nothing and they say very little. One must be in the thing oneself then you can get good and valuable information. I will now send you a telegram with my name and address. Please telegraph me the money it is safer. The newspaper trick is found out and very carefully watched.

CECIL.

Transcription of Rysbach's invisible ink messages used in his trial.

SPYDLE CHALLENGE

Use your language and observation skills to reveal one of the topics covered in the secret messages, mentioned as an inevitable next step in the war. Form the twelve-letter topic word by starting on any letter in the grid below and then tracing a path that spells out the topic by moving only to touching squares, including diagonally touching squares, and without revisiting any square.

Once you've found the topic word, see how many other, shorter words you can find using the same restrictions. Each word must be at least three letters in length, and proper nouns do not count. There are at least 30 more words to be found.

61: BIT BY BIT

The document on the left below, sent by enemy spy Kurt Herlot de Rysbach, demonstrates one way in which invisible ink can be used to communicate a coded message via a newspaper article. In this instance, different letters have been individually highlighted with dots, so that the selected letters spell out a word or message.

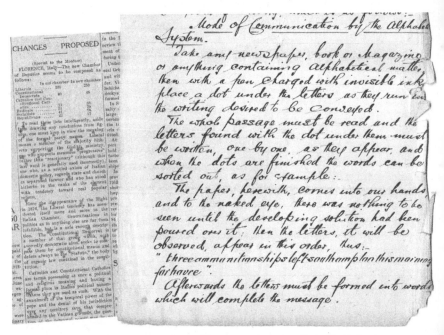

Coded invisible ink message demonstrated by German spy Kurt Herlot de Rysbach.

SPYDLE CHALLENGE

Use your code-cracking and observation skills to decipher the hidden message in the text below. You'll need to use both the text on the left and the symbols on the right to decode it, though how you use them is up to you to work out. Despite its appearance, you *won't* need to use Morse code.

GO HOME SEE	—— —··· —·—
THE TIME AND	·—— —··· ·——
THEN YOU	·——· ———
CAN FIND ME	——— —··— —·

62: THE BITTER END

Carl Friedrick Muller was an enemy spy who was charged
and convicted at the Central Criminal Court with 'feloniously
attempting to communicate and recording and collecting
information with respect to military and naval forces and war
materials with intention of assisting enemy'. He was executed at
the Tower of London on 23 June 1915.

Muller had used invisible ink in his communications, including
on the letter pictured below.

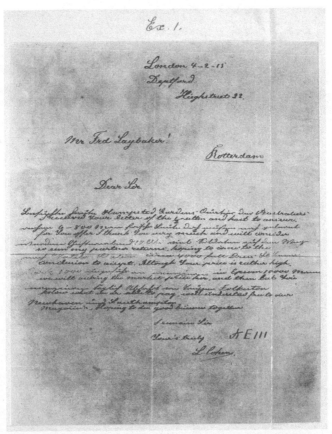

*Letter from German spy Carl Friedrick Muller containing a message
written in invisible ink.*

SPYDLE CHALLENGE

Imagine you have been left in charge of deciphering correspondence which has been sent between two spies who used lemon juice to make some of the material 'invisible'. Use your code-cracking skills to reveal seven different words for military personnel below, one per line. The words have each had any letters also found in the word 'LEMON' removed, so it is up to you to restore these invisible letters.

S DI R

CAD T

FFIC R

R GU AR

S TRY

ARI

RIF   A

63: A DELICATE DANCE

Margaretha Geertruida MacLeod (née Zelle), known professionally as Mata Hari, was a Dutch spy and exotic dancer convicted of spying by France in 1917 and subsequently executed. Her story is said to have inspired the idea of a seductive spy that features in many novels and movies.

Ein Opfer französischen Kriegswahns
MATA HARI
die schöne holländische Tänzerin, die am 15. Oktober 1917
in Frankreich unschuldig erschossen wurde.

German card noting the death of Mata Hari found in Security Service files.

SPYDLE CHALLENGE

Use your code-cracking skills to reveal the name of a world-famous location in which Mata Hari was employed as a dancer. To do so, solve the crossword-style clues and write the resulting words into the numbered boxes. In these boxes each letter has been replaced by a number, with each number always representing the same letter. Once you have identified which letter is represented by every number, you can complete the final row of boxes to reveal the location.

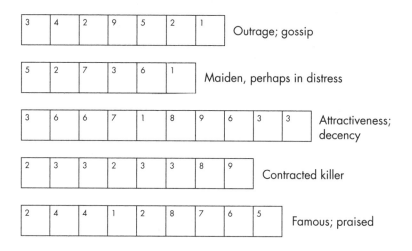

| 3 | 4 | 2 | 9 | 5 | 2 | 1 |
Outrage; gossip

| 5 | 2 | 7 | 3 | 6 | 1 |
Maiden, perhaps in distress

| 3 | 6 | 6 | 7 | 1 | 8 | 9 | 6 | 3 | 3 |
Attractiveness; decency

| 2 | 3 | 3 | 2 | 3 | 3 | 8 | 9 |
Contracted killer

| 2 | 4 | 4 | 1 | 2 | 8 | 7 | 6 | 5 |
Famous; praised

A venue at which Mata Hari performed:

| 1 | 2 | | 3 | 4 | 2 | 1 | 2 | | 5 | 6 |

| 7 | 8 | 1 | 2 | 9 |

You can use the grid below to keep track of your deductions:

| 1 | 2 | 3 | 4 | 5 | 6 | 7 | 8 | 9 |

64: A SEQUENCE OF SPIES

Shown below is a report of alleged meetings and correspondence between Mata Hari and other persons while in France and Spain. Some of the correspondents are given physical descriptions, and often their place of birth is mentioned.

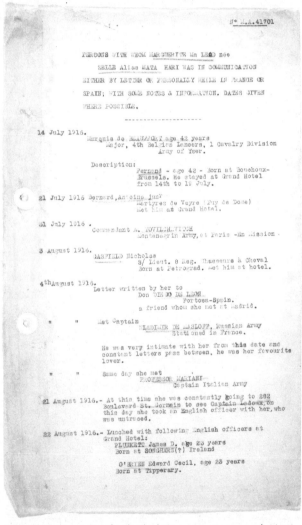

Security Services's list of individuals in communication with Mata Hari between July and August 1917.

SPYDLE CHALLENGE

Imagine you are in charge of collating information about an alleged spy, and want to understand the allegiances of the various people they have met with. You know from which city each of their contacts came, and want to establish the order in which the supposed spy met them. In what order were the contacts from each city met? You know that:

- The contact from Paris was met after, but not immediately after, the Brussels contact
- The Rome contact was met immediately after the person from Smyrna
- The Rome contact was also met later than the contact from Paris
- The person from Smyrna was met before, but not immediately before, the person from Geneva
- After meeting the contact from Dublin, one more person was met prior to meeting the person from Rome
- Similarly, after meeting the contact from Madrid, one more person was met prior to meeting the person from Paris

Number each location with the order in which each of the contacts were met:

Brussels	☐	Milan	☐
Dublin	☐	Paris	☐
Geneva	☐	Rome	☐
Madrid	☐	Smyrna	☐

4 SPIES AND SECRETS

The rise of National Socialism in Germany intensified spy fever in Britain. The German invasion of Poland on 2 September 1939 and Britain's subsequent entry into the Second World War meant that the Security Services now had to deal with the increasing threat of enemy espionage. The training of agents, intelligence gathering, counter-espionage and codebreaking dominated the work of the intelligence services during this time.

Notable academic John Masterman was first drafted into the Intelligence Corps and, after investigating and reporting the Dunkirk evacuations, joined MI5 and soon took control of the Twenty Committee, which ran the Double-Cross System – a British programme to recruit and 'turn', mostly German, agents to work for the Allies during the war. The agents were questioned to reveal the methods used by the Abwehr (German secret service). It was vital to MI5 that communications sent by double agents to Germany were as convincing as possible. The false information they provided formed part of an elaborate and successful deception plan to keep D-Day secret.

The Special Operations Executive (SOE) was formed in June 1940 with the role of promoting sabotage and subversion in enemy-occupied territory and establishing a nucleus of trained men and women tasked with assisting resistance groups there. SOE was run by a chief executive officer who was responsible to the Ministry of Economic Warfare. The organisation ran clandestine networks of agents which typically consisted of a Circuit organiser who took the lead in planning and recruiting new members, a wireless radio operator and a courier. Networks had secret names and often agents had more than one pseudonym. In 1941, SOE became purely a planning and operations organisation.

Many operations during the war required the combined expertise of SOE, MI5 and MI6. For example, the Double-Cross System involved MI5's counter-espionage activities with MI6's foreign intelligence, while SOE's acts of sabotage and resistance across Europe required detailed intelligence from MI6's established networks. Despite the need for cooperation there were tensions between these intelligence organisations; however, each group brought unique capabilities to the table with the shared objective of defeating the Axis powers.

65: TREASURED ASSET

Nathalie Sergueiew, a Russian-born journalist based in Paris, was one of many German agents who double-crossed the Nazi secret service during the Second World War to become an agent for MI5. Her codename was 'Treasure'.

Photo of Second World War double agent Nathalie Sergueiew from Security Service personnel files.

SPYDLE CHALLENGE

Imagine that you are working as part of a counter-espionage department and overseeing the recruitment of double agents. You have received jumbled files concerning four different agents, each of a different nationality. Based on the chart, table and clues below, can you link both the real name and codename of each agent, and say from which city they came?

- The French double agent does not have the codename CRUX
- Eddie Hultz is known as PRINCE
- HERON is either French or is Martha Johannes – but not both
- BLOSSOM is either German or Russian
- CRUX is not German
- Martha Johannes is either German or French
- Jon Merson is Russian
- PRINCE is not French

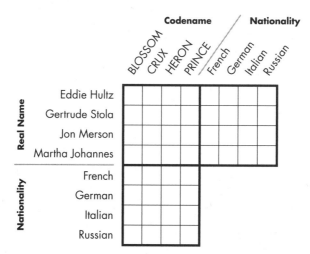

Real Name	Codename	Nationality

66: CARBON COPIES

Treasure, the agent who was double-crossing the Germans, revealed several enemy methods of espionage during interviews with MI5. The document shown below is an official account of what she revealed. One of the methods involved rubbing a carbon pencil over the entirety of a sheet of paper to create a homemade carbon copy paper that could be used to create exact copies of documents.

Third Method

4.   For the other method shown her by DELIDAISE, SERGUEIEW was to take what looked like an indelible copying pencil and with it scribble on a sheet of paper so that one side of it was completely covered. This sheet of paper was then to be used as a carbon. It apparently left no trace on the sheet of paper underneath.

5.   Yvonne DELIDAISE took away SERGUEIEW's experiments in both these methods of secret writing, saying that she would have them developed. SERGUEIEW, however, never saw the results and can give no more information.

Interviewed by Security Services, Sergueiew reveals the instructions given to her by the Germans for secret writing, including this 'third method'.

Use your codebreaking and observation skills to decipher the list of six potential codenames below, all of which are thematically linked in some way. Each codename has, however, been printed twice, creating a 'carbon copy' – and the carbon copies have then been reflected. What are the six codenames, and what is the theme?

CHAOS

ATLAS

URANUS

HYPERION

ARTEMIS

HERA

67: RIGHT-HAND WOMAN

Another method of sending secret correspondence involved
writing invisible messages on the same sheet as otherwise
innocuous cover letters. In this case, the invisible text was written
at ninety degrees relative to the 'cover' letter that had been written
in normal ink.

Fourth Method

6.   The final method of secret writing in which
SERGUEIEW was instructed was that given her for her mission
to this country. For this she was to use the pellets given
her by KLIEMANN before her departure from Paris (see para.112
1st Report). She was instructed in their use in the flat at
29 Avenue de l'Opera (see para.109 1st Report).

7.   A pellet was to be heated in a clear flame which
would not discolour it. When the pellet was melted she was to
take a wooden toothpick and dip it in the liquid. When it
was dry she would re-dip it and continue doing so until all
the liquid had been absorbed and a new pellet reformed on the
end of the stick. This could now be used as pen for her
secret writing. She would then take a sheet of paper (non-
shiny surface) and rub the paper evenly with cotton-wool.
On the side she rubbed she was to write her cover letter in
ink or pencil, preferably the former. Her letter in invisible

N.L.1383
SERGUEIEW, Nathalie   -3-

writing was then to be written on the same side of the paper
but at right angles to the visible text. If SERGUEIEW used
a double sheet which entailed 4 written sides, the invisible
writing was only to be done on the first and third pages.

8.   Her cover letter was to be signed "   ". It
was left to her as to whether she made use of the code for
her invisible writing, but this was considered unnecessary.

Detailed instructions for a fourth method of 'secret writing' Sergueiew was expected to use for secret communications.

SPYDLE CHALLENGE

Use your observation skills to discover a secret message written below. The 'cover' message can be read from left to right, but the 'spy' message is rotated relative to it on the page. What is the secret message?

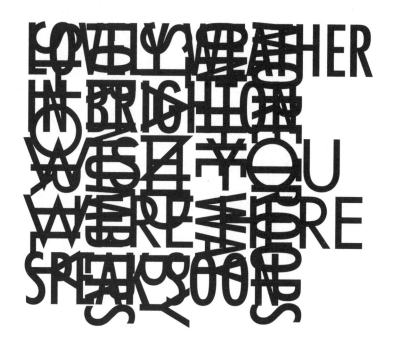

68: A SPY'S SIGN-OFF

Agent Treasure had agreed with her German handlers that any cover letters she sent – hiding otherwise invisible messages – would be signed off with a codename. That way, her messages could be identified as coming from her.

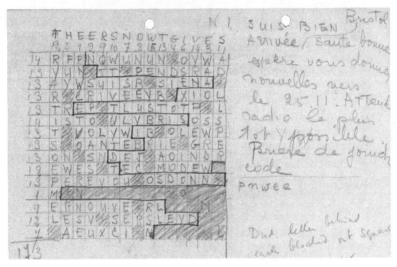

Sergueiew was taught a cipher by her German handler to be used in conjuncture with a book called Montmartre *by Pierre Frondair. She shared this decryption with Security Services.*

SPYDLE CHALLENGE

Crack the number code below to reveal the codename with which Agent Treasure was required to sign off when corresponding with her German handlers. To do so, solve the crossword-style clues and write the resulting words into the numbered boxes. In these boxes each letter has been replaced by a number, with each number always representing the same letter. Once you have identified which letter is represented by every number, you can complete the final row of boxes to reveal the codename.

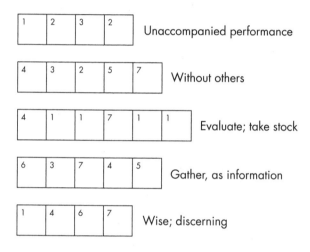

| 1 | 2 | 3 | 2 | | | Unaccompanied performance |

| 4 | 3 | 2 | 5 | 7 | | Without others |

| 4 | 1 | 1 | 7 | 1 | 1 | Evaluate; take stock |

| 6 | 3 | 7 | 4 | 5 | | Gather, as information |

| 1 | 4 | 6 | 7 | | | Wise; discerning |

Agent Treasure's sign-off:

| 1 | 2 | 3 | 4 | 5 | 6 | 7 |

You can use the grid below to keep track of your deductions:

| 1 | 2 | 3 | 4 | 5 | 6 | 7 |

69: LAYING THE TRAIL

Between 1943 and 1945, Agent Treasure's contacts in the German military intelligence service, the Abwehr, believed her to be a loyal German spy. In reality, she was sending them deliberately misleading messages composed by the British Secret Service.

It was vital to MI5 to make the communications sent by double agents to Germany as convincing as possible. The false information they provided formed part of an elaborate and successful deception plan to keep D-Day secret.

Photo of Agent Treasure with her Abwehr handler Major Emil Kliemann, in Lisbon, 1944.

SPYDLE CHALLENGE

Imagine you are a spy handler who is charged with spreading false information in order to confuse enemy secret services. You plan to 'leak' information about three supposed upcoming events, in order to distract the opposition. There will be three coastal decoy locations, each with a different codename. Based on the chart, table and clues below, can you say which decoy locations will be given which codenames, how many troops are said to be due to arrive there, and by what manner?

- It is not the East coast at which 12,000 troops are due to be deployed
- Mobilisation by sea is not part of the plan involving 10,000 troops
- The East coast mobilisation plan is not codenamed WINNER
- TROPHY is either on the North coast or will be targeted by sea – but not both
- WINNER either involves 10,000 troops or the East coast – but not both
- PLATINUM is not the codename for the 12,000-troop deployment
- Troop mobilisation by air is not part of the plan codenamed WINNER

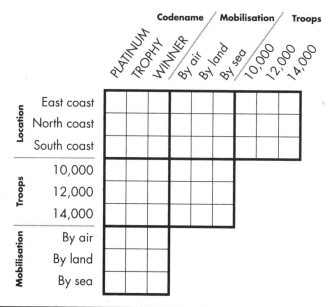

Location	Codename	Troops	Mobilisation

70: HIGH PRAISE

Agent Treasure's notable efforts in helping to deceive enemy forces and her assistance in providing information to help decode the enemy's encrypted correspondence were acknowledged in the letter below. The letter was sent to John Cecil Masterman, a key player in the Double-Cross arrangement.

Original in SF. 51/32/24(6)

COPY

TOP SECRET

G.C. & C.S.

26th May, 1944.

My dear J.C.,

    I should like you and Robertson to know how much we appreciate the assistance you are giving us in respect of TRAMP/TREASURE and BRUTUS/HUBERT traffic. I have discussed the matter again this morning with the people actually on the job, and I find that about 30% of our success with the whole French network has been due solely to TRAMP and HUBERT: experience in using the material will certainly raise this proportion even higher.

    It is seldom that we get such a stroke of luck in this job, especially with traffic so valuable as our French network: so I thought it right that you should know what a high degree of importance we at this end attribute to BRUTUS and TREASURE.

(Sgd.)   Denys Page.

Assistant Director.

Major J.C. Masterman,
M.I.5.

Letter regarding Sergueiew's important work as a double agent.

SPYDLE CHALLENGE

The letter opposite was from Denys Page, whose place of work is shown at the top of the page only as 'G.C. & C.S.'. Use your tracking skills to spell out the full name of the department this letter was sent from by starting on the grey square below, then tracing a path that visits every grid square. As it travels, the path must spell out the name of the department, whose initials match the ones printed on the letter. The path can only travel horizontally or vertically between squares.

As a bonus challenge, can you say what this department is now known as?

71: A LITTLE OFF-TRACK

Treasure was an effective double agent, but according
to Masterman – the architect of the Double-Cross System –
she was also 'exceptionally temperamental and troublesome'. In
conversations with her MI5 handler, Mary Sherer, Treasure
revealed that she had let slip her double identity to an American
soldier with whom she had had an affair. She also threatened to
stop working for MI5 unless they arranged for her beloved pet
dog, Babs, to join her. However, Babs had to be left behind when
she began her mission in England.

In this document, Colonel Robertson, Sherer's boss, records
the angry meeting he had with Treasure in which he told her that
her services were no longer required, because her behaviour was
endangering the Allies.

```
                          TREASURE
                          --------

          Yesterday I saw TREASURE at 39 Hill Street in the
    presence of Miss Sherer.

          I said that I had come to deliver a very serious talk
    as I had, during the past few days, formed definite opinions
    with regard to her case.   I said that we had already taken
    over the transmitter and were imitating her and that in future she
    would not be required to assist us in this way.   I pointed out
    that my reasons for coming to this conclusion were two-fold:

              (1)   that I had heard from Miss Sherer that TREASURE
                    had been to Lisbon in order to fix up with
Pr ¢ 66 182        KLIEMANN a signal or signals which would appear
                    in her messages indicating whether or not she was
                    working under control, and

              (2)   that from a reliable source it had been reported
                    that while in Lisbon she had fixed up a means of
                    communication with a German Intelligence Officer
                    without this coming to our notice.

          I pointed out that it was quite impossible for me to place
    any confidence in someone who behaved in this manner.
```

Security Services report by Colonel Robertson.

SPYDLE CHALLENGE

Reveal the place where Treasure had to leave her dog, Babs, by placing A, B, D, G, I, L, R, T, or S into each empty square, so that no letter repeats in any row, column or bold-lined 3×3 box. Once solved, the name of the location can be read down the shaded diagonal.

	A	B		D		S		
L				S				G
			L		G	D		
I		G				A		T
	R						D	
S		A				R		I
		I	S		R			
D				G				S
	L		T		A		I	

72: THE PRICE OF LOYALTY

In the lead up to D-Day, Treasure admitted, threateningly, she had agreed a secret signal with her Abwehr (German military intelligence) contact, Emil Kliemann, so he would know if her transmissions were genuine. This meant that if another agent took over her transmissions her cover would be blown, putting at risk the whole network of double agents.

Regretting her outburst, an upset Treasure met with her MI5 handler, Mary Sherer, and wrote down the secret code that she had agreed with Kleinman. This is that original note.

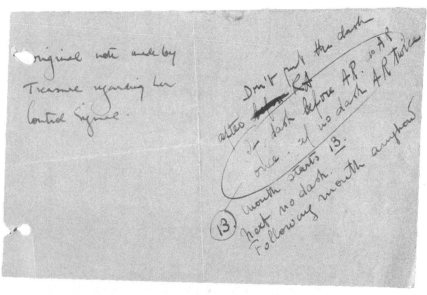

Treasure's note revealing her secret code signal.

SPYDLE CHALLENGE

During the heated meeting with her handler's boss, Colonel Robertson –
described in the previous puzzle – Treasure was offered a weekly sum of
money, despite being ostensibly removed from operations.

To calculate the weekly sum she was offered, start with the number at
the top of the chain below, then follow the arrows to apply each operation
in turn until you reach the 'TOTAL' box. Write your answer at the bottom.
As an extra Spydle challenge, try to do the entire calculation in your head,
without writing anything down until you reach the final TOTAL area.

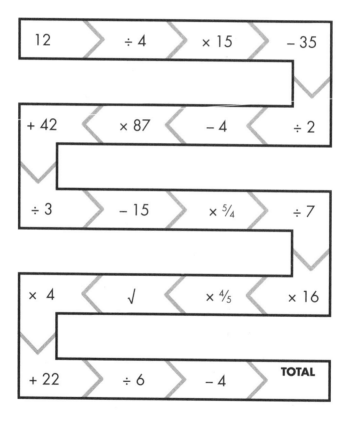

How much was Treasure offered per week after the meeting, in pounds?

73: CROSSING THE LINE

Edward Arnold Chapman, codenamed Zigzag, had been a burglar and expert safe-blower before the Second World War. Imprisoned for his crimes, he remained in prison on Jersey during the occupation. Having offered his services to them as a spy, he was trained, equipped and later dropped by parachute near Ely, Cambridgeshire. He immediately sought to tell the British authorities about his recruitment by the Nazis and was taken on by MI5 as a double agent.

Chapman's training by the Germans had been as a sabotage agent. He had been supplied with money and explosives and tasked with sabotaging the de Havilland aircraft factory at Hatfield, Hertfordshire.

Edward Chapman, Agent "Zigzag" 1944

SPYDLE CHALLENGE

Use your code-cracking skills to reveal the name of the aircraft which was being made at the de Havilland factory at the time of the planned sabotage. To do so, solve the crossword-style clues and write the resulting words into the numbered boxes. In these boxes each letter has been replaced by a number, with each number always representing the same letter. Once you have identified which letter is represented by which number, you can complete the final row of boxes to reveal the aircraft name.

| 2 | 1 | 6 | 7 | Leave out |

| 4 | 5 | 6 | 7 | Give up something |

| 1 | 2 | 7 | 7 | 2 | Slogan |

| 2 | 5 | 3 | 7 | Expel |

| 3 | 5 | 1 | 1 | 6 | 7 | Mountain peak |

Name of the aircraft manufactured at the de Havilland factory:

| 1 | 2 | 3 | 4 | 5 | 6 | 7 | 2 |

You can use the grid below to keep track of your deductions:

| 1 | 2 | 3 | 4 | 5 | 6 | 7 |

74: A TALE OF DECEIT

After the successful 'sabotage' of the de Havilland factory, Zigzag prepared to be sent back to his German handlers. Before his return, he was subject to 'practice' interrogations, to make sure his account of the falsified events was watertight.

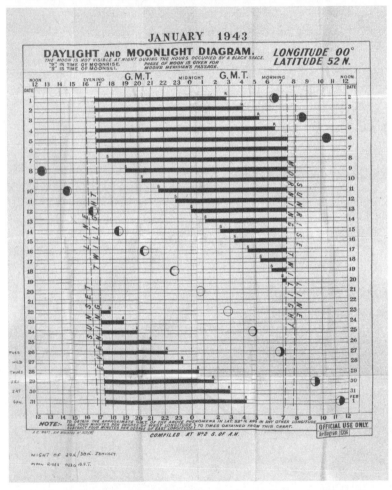

Moon calendar for January 1943, used to perfect the timings for when Zigzag's 'bombing' on the de Havilland took place.

SPYDLE CHALLENGE

Imagine that you are about to be tested with a false interrogation, to make sure your story stacks up when the other side interrogates you for real. You need to account for your activities over the last few weeks, and must present them in a consistent order. Based on the following statements you have made, can you label the exact order you are claiming to have undertaken these in?

- Falsifying documents was the next thing you did after the dead letter drop
- The reconnaissance was after but not immediately after the language class
- Falsifying documents was the last thing you did
- You met with the handler immediately after fitness training
- Comms interception came immediately before the language class
- The dead letter drop was immediately after filing a case report

Number each activity with the order in which you are claiming it took place:

Comms interception ☐   Fitness training ☐

Dead letter drop ☐   Language class ☐

Falsifying documents ☐   Meeting with handler ☐

Filing case report ☐   Reconnaissance ☐

75: SELF-SABOTAGE

The double agent codenamed Zigzag returned to his German controllers in 1943, via Lisbon. He was awarded the Iron Cross, the Nazi award for gallantry, following his success in arranging the 'attack' on the de Havilland aircraft factory that had in fact been concocted by MI5.

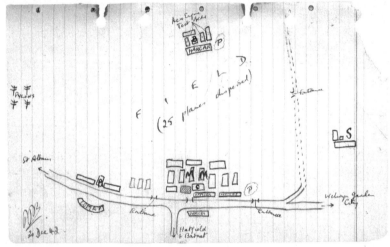

Sketch of the de Havilland factory included in Zigzag's report of his visit there.

Photo showing MI5's fake sabotage of the de Havilland factory.

SPYDLE CHALLENGE

Imagine you are a double agent needing to give a false report on an act of sabotage you are supposed to have been essential to – but which is entirely invented. It's important to get your story straight so that you don't blow your cover. So far, your report suggests:

- The North wing is the site of either the collapsed ceiling or the hole in the outer wall
- The arson did not cause the smoke damage
- The North wing was not the site of the arson attack
- The collapsed ceiling was caused by a burst water main
- The electricity cables were not cut in the main warehouse

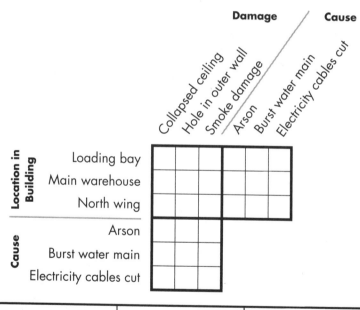

Location in Building	Damage	Cause

76: LOOSE CANNON

In June 1944, Edward Arnold Chapman, the double agent known as Zigzag, was again dropped by parachute, this time charged by the Germans with espionage on military targets and to report on V-bomb damage. Once back in England, Chapman gave his British handlers much useful information about Germany. By October 1944, however, MI5 had discovered that Chapman had, despite his denials, shared details of his role as spy and counter-spy with friends, some of whom were former criminals. The case was discontinued as a result. He later published his own account of his wartime exploits in a book.

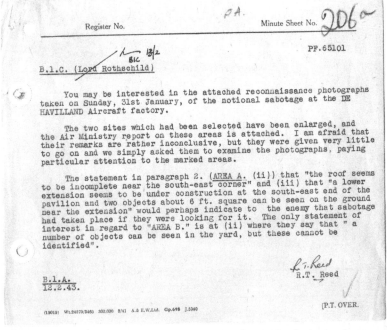

Accompanying note to reconnaissance photos taken by MI5 for the 'notional sabotage at the de Havilland factory'.

SPYDLE CHALLENGE

Imagine that you are the handler of a double agent who is believed to have spilled secrets about their identity and mission to others. You need to work out what information has been released, and to whom. There are four people to whom your agent has given information, each of a different nationality. Each has also been assigned their own codename. Can you complete the table below with information on all four of these people, based on the chart and the following clues?

- The Dutch person did not receive the report of a previous mission
- The French recipient was told about the name of the agent's handler
- The plans for the next mission were sent to the person codenamed Blunt
- The report of a previous mission was not sent to Tricky
- Agent Marrow is either Dutch or French
- Agent Cooper is not Norwegian
- The name of the agent's handler was not sent to Marrow

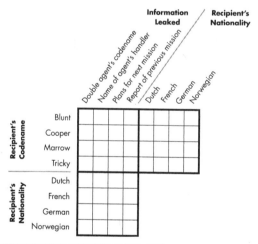

Recipient's Codename	Information Leaked	Recipient's Nationality

77: HE SAID, HE SAID

Welsh-born Agent Snow was recruited by the Special Intelligence
Service (MI6) in 1936, but also reported to German intelligence
(Abwehr) without MI6's knowledge. After being cautioned, he
voluntarily deposited an Abwehr radio set at Victoria Station.
He continued to work for the Security Service until March 1941,
when on a flight back from Lisbon with Agent Celery he claimed
he had been confronted by his Abwehr controllers. He was
carrying with him £10,000 and explosive pens.

Agent Celery was sent by MI5 into Germany to infiltrate the
Abwehr by offering the Germans intelligence and persuading
them that he was a traitor. Snow believed that Celery had
been 'turned'. Upon their return to England, they were both
interrogated. Their stories did not match and despite MI5's
conflicting opinions it was Snow who was subsequently interned
until September 1944.

Transcription of Agent Snow's interrogation of Agent Celery.

SPYDLE CHALLENGE

Imagine you are responsible for three agents, one of whom has betrayed the other two. They are known by their codenames, which are Frank, Russet and Milton. You know that: one of them always lies; one of them always tells the truth; and one of them sometimes lies and sometimes tells the truth. You need to work out which is which. When you ask each of them for the truth, this is what they say:

> **FRANK:** I always tell the truth, but the same can't be said for Milton. He sometimes tells the truth, but I know he sometimes lies too.

> **RUSSET:** Frank will pretend to be innocent in all this but I know he's in the habit of telling lies. He throws a few truths in the mix, though, to make sure nobody is too suspicious.

> **MILTON:** I can't speak for Russet, but I know Frank will lie to you. Sure, he might tell you the truth as well — but he lies sometimes.

You know that the traitor is the one who lies all the time. Who is it?

78: RESPONSIBLE OFFICER

Born to Jewish parents and Romanian by birth, Vera Atkins was educated in Paris and London. Her mother was British so she was able to emigrate to Britain in 1937 with the help of British intelligence diplomats who vouched for her commitment to Britain. Nine months after it was formed, Vera Atkins joined SOE's French section in April 1941 as an intelligence officer. She handled over 400 agents, of whom many were women. She coordinated missions from Britain, never experiencing being in the field. After the war she travelled to Europe to try to trace the missing agents who had not returned.

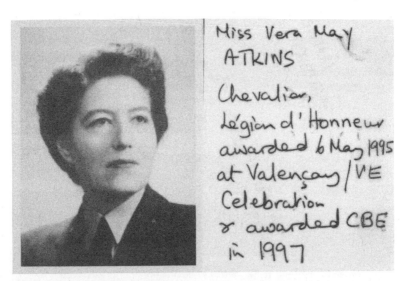

Miss Vera May ATKINS
Chevalier, Légion d'Honneur
awarded 6 May 1995 at Valençay/VE Celebration
& awarded CBE in 1997

SOE photo of WAAF Squadron Officer Vera Atkins.

SPYDLE CHALLENGE

Imagine you are responsible for the coordination of four secret agents, and must make sure that each agent is equipped for their next mission. Each of the agents has been assigned to a different mission, but there are some administrative tasks for you to oversee before each one can depart. Based on the following clues, along with the chart, complete the table below to show each agent's codename alongside their mission codename and the task that you must complete first.

- UNDERMINE is either the mission codename for AZALEA, or is the mission that requires false visas to be issued – but not both
- A flight must be arranged for mission FLUMMOX
- MAGNOLIA is assigned to mission FLUMMOX
- VERONICA is either on mission DISCOMBOBULATE or requires a flight arranged – but not both
- Mission DISCOMBOBULATE does not need a passport provided
- Procuring an enemy uniform is required for UNDERMINE

Agent Codename	Mission Codename	Task to Complete

79: KEEPING MUM

The Special Operation Executive's security training school organised schemes all over Britain for would-be agents. They laid traps to test their resilience and suitability for missions.

Marie Christine Chilver, codenamed Fifi, was a special asset to SOE's training programme as she was used to test the trustworthiness of new SOE recruits. Recruits expecting to meet a contact during their training missions encountered instead a stunning blonde claiming to be a French freelance journalist named Christine Collard.

Using her skills of character assessment, intelligence and courage, Fifi listened carefully and conversed with the students at length, assessing them for suitability for the service.

During the war, anti-gossip posters were created by the Central Office of Information to warn anyone of spreading sensitive information.

SPYDLE CHALLENGE

Use your linguistic skills to reveal the name given to Agent Fifi's missions to extract information from unwitting students. Jumbled up in the circle below are the letters which spell out the name of the technique, which can be formed by using each letter exactly once.

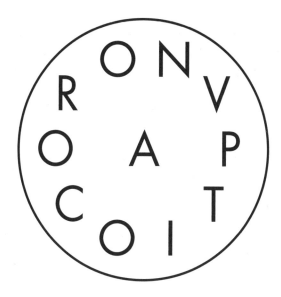

How many additional words can you find in the circle? Each word must use the centre letter plus two or more of the other letters, but no letter may be used more times than it appears within the circle. There are over 60 additional words to find, not including proper nouns.

80: SPILLING THE BEANS

A brush with femme fatale Fifi could mean a promising student's downfall. José Tinchant, a talented young Belgian, was highly regarded by his instructors until his encounter with Fifi. She reported back to SOE the sorry details of their first meeting, saying, '*by the evening I had learnt practically all there was to know about him.*' Tinchant's file reveals that he wasted much of his available time in Fifi's company. Unimpressed, SOE ended Tinchant's training employment.

Don't forget that walls have ears!
Careless Talk Costs Lives campaign

SPYDLE CHALLENGE

Imagine that you have been tasked with testing agents-in-training to see if they give away sensitive information. Four meetings with trainees so far have resulted in a 'success', in so much as you have learned their real first names, codenames, ages and the destinations they are due to be dispatched to. Use the clues and chart below to gather your findings and fill out the table beneath to record what each agent has told you.

- Mark is being sent to Paris
- The 21-year-old does not have the codename Cricket
- John is not also known as Cricket
- The 24-year-old is either codenamed Penguin or Banjo
- Antwerp is not where John is going
- Peter is either going to Calais or is 21 – but not both
- Charles is not also called Marble
- Cricket is not the codename of the 22-year-old
- Peter is known as Penguin
- Charles is either 21 or is codenamed Penguin

Real Forename	Codename	Age	Destination

81: MAKING CONTACT

Krystyna Skarbek's Secret Service file describes her as a *'flaming patriot, expert skier and great adventuress'*. When Germany invaded her homeland of Poland on 1 September 1939, she was in South Africa. Shocked by the news, she travelled by steamer from Cape Town to Southampton and demanded that she be taken on by the British Secret Service. Also known as Christine Granville, she assumed many identities and was reputed to have had many admirers and lovers, but, more significantly, gathered a vast amount of intelligence from Nazi-occupied territories that significantly benefited the Allies. Known for her courage and fearlessness and for her risky missions to Nazi-occupied Poland and France during the war, she was regarded by many as Churchill's favourite spy.

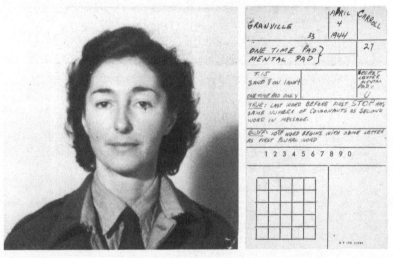

Photo of SOE agent Christine Granville and her code card.

SPYDLE CHALLENGE

Use your code-cracking skills to reveal the name of a Polish underground resistance group with whom Granville made contact when she was working as a spy. To do so, solve the crossword-style clues and write the resulting words into the numbered boxes. In these boxes each letter has been replaced by a number, with each number always representing the same letter. Once you have identified which letter is represented by every number, you can complete the final row of boxes to reveal the name of the resistance group.

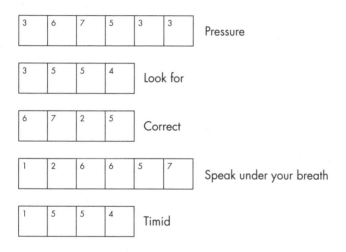

| 3 | 6 | 7 | 5 | 3 | 3 |

Pressure

| 3 | 5 | 5 | 4 |

Look for

| 6 | 7 | 2 | 5 |

Correct

| 1 | 2 | 6 | 6 | 5 | 7 |

Speak under your breath

| 1 | 5 | 5 | 4 |

Timid

Name of the Polish underground network:

| 1 | 2 | 3 | 4 | 5 | 6 | 5 | 5 | 7 | 3 |

You can use the grid below to keep track of your working out:

| 1 | 2 | 3 | 4 | 5 | 6 | 7 |

82: THE MOTIVE

Noor Inayat Khan was a young, gentle-mannered WAAF
(Women's Auxiliary Air Force) officer who was recruited by Vera
Atkins in May 1943. Despite some training officers' doubts of
her suitability for SOE, Vera never questioned her commitment
and thought she was ideal in that she could easily pose as a
Frenchwoman, as Paris had been her childhood home and where
she had been educated. Noor became the first female wireless
operator to be sent to France.

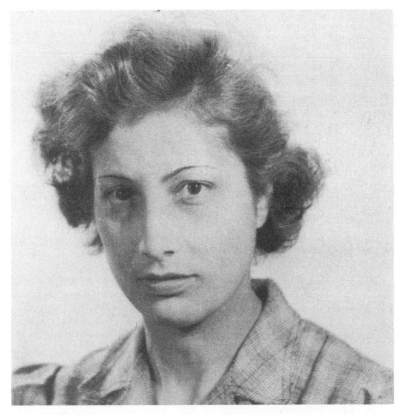

Noor Inayat Khan

SPYDLE CHALLENGE

Transcribed below is an extract from a report on Khan's time as an officer student. Some words have been written in upper case, and these are to be placed into the grid so that they read either across or down, one letter per box and ignoring hyphens. Once complete, rearrange the letters in the shaded squares to reveal Khan's supposed motive for her war work, according to the report. What was it?

'She is, also, very FEMININE in character, very EAGER to please, very READY to ADAPT herself to the MOOD of the COMPANY, or the TONE of the CONVERSATION, INTERESTED in PERSONALITIES, CAPABLE of strong ATTACHMENTS, KIND-HEARTED, EMOTIONAL and IMAGINATIVE.'

83: WIRELESS MISSIONS

By 1943 the life expectancy of a wireless operator during the Second World War was approximately six weeks. Noor landed in northern France on the night of 16 June 1943 and joined the network called 'Prosper'. Only a week later the Germans infiltrated the network and began rounding up the agents. Noor had the opportunity to fly back to London but chose to remain in Paris, maintaining radio contact with London until her arrest in early October 1943. She escaped from Nazi headquarters in Paris in November but was recaptured and imprisoned. After the war Vera Atkins uncovered the fate of 117 missing agents, of which one was Noor.

```
        This officer, went to the Field on 16th June 1943,
as a W/T operator to one of our most important organisers.
Shortly after her arrival the Gestapo became extremely active
in her area.   Her group was penetrated and, on the arrest
of the organiser and his chief Lieutenants, it finally
collapsed.
```

Extract of report from Noor Inayat Khan's SOE personnel file.

SPYDLE CHALLENGE

Imagine that you are a spy using wireless technology to communicate enemy information back to your superiors. There are four codenamed correspondents who you communicate with, each of whom requires a specific 'pass' word from you so that they know your transmission is genuine. Each of them is also based in a different British city. Use the clues below, and the information in the chart, to work out which correspondent is located where, and what 'pass' word each requires.

- The person in London uses the 'pass' word Windbreak
- WHITTLE's 'pass' word is not Tenacity
- FARRIER is either in Liverpool or requires you to mention 'Hijinks' – but not both
- 'Hijinks' is not used by WHITTLE
- MORTON is not the correspondent who needs you to reference 'Tenacity'
- WHITTLE is not in London
- MORTON is in Birmingham

Codename	'Pass' Word	City

84: A WOMAN OF MANY NAMES

Virginia Hall was an American who was an agent for the SOE and the American Office of Strategic Services. An expert in coding and decoding telegrams before the war, she found herself in Europe when war was declared. Not wishing to return home, she chose to stay and find a purpose in the war effort. Despite having only one leg she was recruited in London by the French Section of SOE. She infiltrated the Vichy command in France and became a prime target of the Gestapo.

Photos from SOE agent Virginia Hall's personnel file.

SPYDLE CHALLENGE

The names and nicknames encoded below are all associated with Virginia Hall. In each case they have been disguised by using a Caesar shift in which each letter has been 'shifted' forwards by a fixed number of positions through the alphabet. With a shift of +1, for example, A would become B, B would become C, and so on until Z became A.

Crack the code to reveal the codenames and nicknames, all of which have been encoded with the same shift.

Codename in the field:

RFWNJ

Nickname she gave to her prosthetic leg:

HZYMGJWY

Nickname given to her by the Germans:

YMJ QNRUNSL QFID

Additional nickname given to her by the Germans:

FWYJRNX

Nickname given to her by fellow SOE agents:

RFWNJ TK QDTS

Codename used by downed airmen when seeking her help:

TQNANJW

85: WHAT'S IN A NAME?

The Special Operations Executive (SOE) trained their agents to use quick disguises in looks and behaviour so they could easily change their characteristics. They had been drilled to have cover stories in the event of interrogation and used codenames and aliases to hide their identities. An SOE agent and a member of the French Resistance, Eliane Plewman, used a cover name and three codenames during her time as a courier in occupied France.

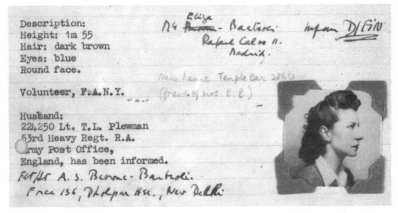

SOE personnel report record on Eliane Sophie Plewman, née Brown-Bartroli.

SPYDLE CHALLENGE

Use the chart and clues below to match up three of the female SOE agents, Eliane Plewman, Noor Inayat Khan and Virginia Hall, with their real-life codenames and cover surnames. Their 'field' names were one-word codenames, and they were also given false surnames associated with their cover story. Can you fill out the table with the correct information?

- Diane was not the field name of Noor Inayat Khan
- Montagne was not a cover surname for Eliane Plewman
- Eliane Plewman either used the file name Gaby or had a cover surname of Renier, but not both
- The field name Diane was not used by the person with the cover surname of Renier
- The surname Renier was not used by Eliane Plewman

		Field Name			Cover Surname		
		Diane	Gaby	Madeleine	Montagne	Prunier	Renier
Real Name	Eliane Plewman						
	Noor Inayat Khan						
	Virginia Hall						
Cover Surname	Montagne						
	Prunier						
	Renier						

Real Name	Field Name	Cover Surname

5 BEHIND ENEMY LINES

Working behind enemy lines is one of the riskiest activities in intelligence gathering; the documents, maps and gadgets designed to aid the spy's mission can quickly turn into incriminating evidence. This was exactly what happened to German agent Karel Richter, who was captured soon after being parachuted into Britain during the Second World War. The stakes were high; Richter was charged under the Treachery Act of 1940 and found guilty. On 10 December 1941 he was hanged at Wandsworth Prison.

Other forms of reconnaissance in the Second World War were conducted through branches of the armed forces, rather than intelligence services. For example, the Long Range Desert Group (LRDG), as the name suggests, was a unit of the British army specialising in desert warfare. This meant that the LRDG was capable not just of intelligence gathering, but also of carrying out raids in their heavily armed vehicles. Their intelligence reports, particularly on Axis traffic on the routes from Tripoli to Benghazi, were vital to the success of the Western Desert campaign. This campaign had begun in 1940 and culminated in Allied victory at the battle of El Alamein in late 1942, followed by the surrender of Axis forces in North Africa in early 1943.

This could be on a grand scale. Operation Fortitude South aimed to deceive the Germans into believing that the Allied invasion of France would come through the Pas-de-Calais, the part of France closest to Britain. Fortitude North was designed to feign an Allied build-up directed at occupied Norway. Accordingly, fictional armies were 'assembled' in the Kent countryside and around Edinburgh. The southern field armies were replete with inflatable tanks, landing craft and other field equipment.

The end of the Second World War brought an uneasy peace, with Europe divided between the capitalist west and communist east. The two sides met in Cold War Berlin, a hotbed of espionage and intrigue, and a microcosm of the Cold War itself. Here, a hundred miles into communist East Germany, was a city divided into two. East Berlin was administered by East Germany, while West Berlin was a de facto enclave of West Germany and enjoyed the freedoms and economic prosperity that capitalism afforded. The construction of a wall around West Berlin in 1961 by the East German authorities, to prevent the flow of East Germans seeking a better life in the west, severely strained superpower relations. This was the tense environment that Britain's military liaison mission, known as BRIXMIS, operated in. Its intelligence gathering continued up until the end of the Cold War and was mirrored by Soviet spying in West Germany. BRIXMIS, mapped Soviet military installations, photographed military vehicles and aircraft and even recovered the engines of a Soviet fighter jet that had crashed in a lake near Berlin. However, by the 1980s communism was in a state of crisis, unable to deliver improving living standards or basic freedoms that were taken for granted in the west. On 9 November 1989, the crossing points through the Berlin Wall were opened, precipitating the wall's demise and the end of the Cold War era of espionage.

86: OVERHEAD OPERATIONS

Photographic intelligence was used to detect and destroy the launch sites of German V1 'flying bombs' and V2 rockets from 1943 to 1945. The photos were interpreted at the Central Interpretation Unit at RAF Medmenham, using stereoscopic methods – these made it easier to locate the narrow ramps that were used to launch V1s, as they would otherwise blend into the terrain.

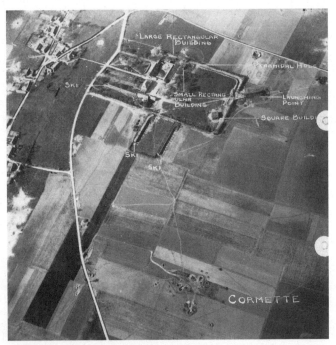

Aerial reconnaissance photograph of the hamlet of Cormette, 6 km west of Saint-Omer, in northern France.

SPYDLE CHALLENGE

Use your visual perspective interpretation skills to reveal the name of the operation described opposite, which relied on aerial intelligence. Imagine looking down on each of the structures below, looking first along the top row from left to right and then the bottom row from left to right. What eight-letter word is spelled out by the structures, as pictured from a bird's-eye view directly above them?

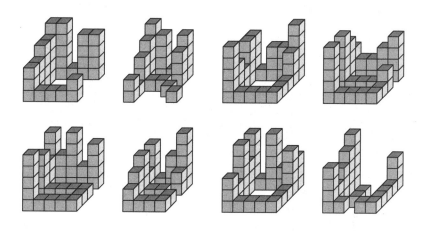

87: UNDER THE RADAR

The *Tirpitz* was a German battleship destroyed by the RAF in Operation Catechism on 12 November 1944. *Tirpitz* was camouflaged in a Norwegian fjord and posed such a threat to Allied convoys that several attempts were made to sink the vessel, culminating in the successful Catechism raid. Aerial photo reconnaissance and intelligence played a vital part in locating the *Tirpitz*.

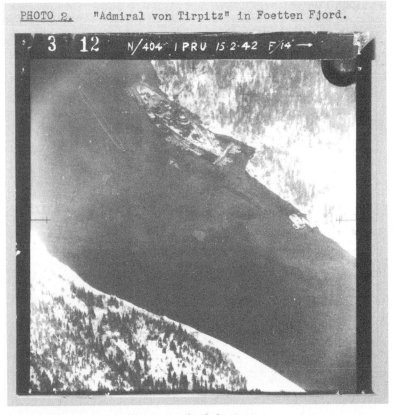

PHOTO 2.   "Admiral von Tirpitz" in Foetten Fjord.

3 12 N/404 I PRU 15·2·42 F/14 →

Naval intelligence photo of the German battleship Tirpitz.

SPYDLE CHALLENGE

The names of ten military vehicles, including naval vessels, have been given below. The names, however, are camouflaged among geographical features. Uncover the vehicles by crossing out the letters in the overlapping features. For example, the line 'HCIARLL' has a 'CAR' camouflaged by a 'HILL'. The letters on each line are always in the correct order for both words.

TCOAVNEK

ADRRCEHAIDPNELOAUGGHOT

SMUOUBMANRTIANEIN

WVOALRCSAHINPO

ACEANROYPLOANEN

GFUJNOBORATD

HGELLAICOCIPETERR

ISDETSHTRMOUYSER

MIISNESWLEAENPEDR

SLAEAGPOLOANEN

88: LONG-RANGE MISSIONS

The Long Range Desert Group (LRDG) was an intelligence-gathering, reconnaissance and raiding unit of the British army during the Second World War. It was formed in July 1940 under Major Ralph Bagnold, and operated primarily in North Africa.

Photograph of an LRDG patrol in the Western Desert in Africa.

SPYDLE CHALLENGE

Imagine you are putting together an intelligence report, based on information you have received from agents behind enemy lines. They have sent information about the numbers of troops and assets at four different locations, each of which has been given a codename. You also know that:

- The gun battery is not at the place where 1,000 troops are posted
- The anti-tank guns are not at the site codenamed LYNX
- Neither the tanks nor the gun battery are at the site of 1,200 troops
- The site with 2,400 troops also has aircraft
- The gun battery is at the location codenamed PANTHER
- The site with aircraft is known as THORN

Use the clues and the chart to complete the table showing how many troops are posted at each location, and with what assets.

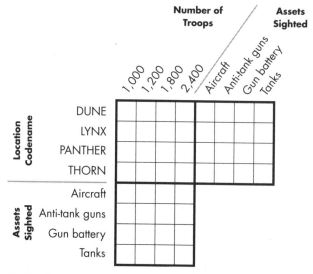

Location Codename	Number of Troops	Assets Sighted

89: SPECIAL SERVICES

Due to the Long Range Desert Group's (LRDG) mastery of desert navigation and reconnaissance, their role soon expanded to include offensive action. They assisted other special forces, such as the Special Air Service (SAS), which relied on them for transport to their targets.

Publicity photograph showing the LRDG carrying out surveillance in the Western Desert.

SPYDLE CHALLENGE

The LRDG's assistance in the newly formed SAS's missions earned them a humorous nickname. Use your tracking skills to discover the nickname, which is hidden in the grid below, by starting on the grey square and tracing a path that visits every grid square. As it travels, the path must spell out the nickname, which consists of four separate words. The path can only travel horizontally or vertically between squares.

	I	C	E
L	V	R	E
I	B	Y	S
D	N	A	I
E	R	T	X
S	E	T	A

90: TERMS OF ENGAGEMENT

The SAS was conceived by a commando, Lieutenant David
Stirling, and the unit was subsequently approved by the army
High Command. The intention was for the group to parachute in
behind enemy lines to carry out small-scale offensives. Below is
an extract from their war diary for D-Day, 6 June 1944.

Extract from the intelligence summary, or war diary, of the HQ SAS troops for D-Day.

SPYDLE CHALLENGE

Stirling was given a nickname by German forces who had heard of his covert operations.

Use your code-cracking skills to reveal this nickname by solving the crossword-style clues and writing the resulting words into the numbered boxes. In these boxes each letter has been replaced by a number, with each number always representing the same letter. Once you have identified which letter is represented by every number, you can complete the final row of boxes to reveal the nickname.

8	3	1	3	4

Second World War adversary

1	2	3	9	3	6	2

Ancient Egyptian ruler

9	3	1	1	6	9	5

Harmonious relationship

1	3	9	3	5	9	6	6	1

Adjective for SAS air soldiers

1	3	4	6	9	3	7	3

Wide, unbroken view

Stirling's nickname:

1	2	3	4	5	6	7

7	3	8	6	9

You can use the grid below to keep track of your working out:

1	2	3	4	5	6	7	8	9

91: HARD LANDING

Enemy spies sometimes parachuted into Britain. Karel Richter was one such agent of the German intelligence service. The image shown below is a newspaper cutting reporting Richter's capture, and subsequent execution. According to the report, Richter had parachuted into London Colney in Hertfordshire, along with several incriminating items suggesting his links to German intelligence.

WAR P.C. TRAPS GERMAN IN 20 MIN. SPY DRAMA

A GERMAN spy who landed in this country by parachute was captured twenty minutes after leaving his hide-out by the prompt action of a policeman.

Karel Richard Richter, 29, who was executed at Wandsworth Gaol yesterday, was leaving a wood near the village of London Colney, Hertfordshire, on May 14, when a lorry driver, who had lost his way, hailed him.

The driver got no help from Richter, who moved on.

At this moment War Reserve Police-Constable Alec John Scott appeared. The driver made a casual remark about the unhelpful stranger.

This aroused the suspicions of Police-Constable Scott, who went after Richter, then only twelve yards away. Questions followed. Soon a police patrol car was speeding to the scene.

News clipping from a Daily Mirror article on Karel Richter, in December 1941, found in his Secret Service file.

SPYDLE CHALLENGE

Another part of the newspaper clipping, not shown opposite, details the items which Richter had hastily buried upon his landing. Use your tracking skills to reveal the list of items, as given in the article. Starting on the top-left square below, find a path that visits every grid square. As it travels, the path must spell out the names of the seven items. The path can only travel horizontally or vertically between squares, and will finish at the bottom-left square. Fill in the item list beneath, one letter per underline, as you solve.

P	A	R	R	N	E	S	S
N	I	A	A	H	E	R	C
G	Y	C	H	U	T	A	S
S	L	F	T	E	M	L	H
U	P	I	S	T	O	E	H
I	T	A	R	T	L	F	O
E	T	N	S	L	R	A	O
R	T	I	M	E	C	P	D

Items discovered:

_ _ _ _ _ _ _ _

_ _ _ _ _ _

_ _ _ _   _ _ _ _ _ _

_ _ _ _ _   _ _ _ _

_ _ _ _ _ _

_ _ _ _   _ _ _ _ _ _

_ _ _ _ _ _ _ _ _ _

92: SUFFICIENT SUPPLIES

German spy Karel Richter was questioned after a lorry driver who had stopped by chance to ask him for directions reported the appearance of an injured foreigner to the local police. According to a police report, Richter had brought many personal effects with him, as well as the intelligence-related items which he had attempted to bury.

Secret Service photos of the search where German spy Karel Richter had disclosed he had hidden his parachute and apparatus.

SPYDLE CHALLENGE

Place each of these personal items, all of which were listed as Richter's possessions in the police report, into the grid below, writing one letter per box. All of the entries must be spelled out either from left to right or top to bottom. Ignore any spaces when doing so. Once complete, the letters in the highlighted squares can be arranged to spell out the name of the location (2, 6) of the police station which filed the report.

3-letter word
MAP

4-letter word
PIPE

5-letter words
KNIFE
PURSE
RAZOR

6-letter words
ID CARD
MIRROR
PENCIL
WALLET

7-letter words
LIGHTER
TOBACCO

8-letter words
NAIL FILE
PASSPORT

11-letter word
FOUNTAIN PEN

12-letter words
HANDKERCHIEF
SHAVING STICK

93: LOCATED IN PART

Among German agent Karel Richter's possessions was a map of part of the east of England. According to the MI5 report filed on the spy, he claimed to have already visited several places in East Anglia by the time he was questioned.

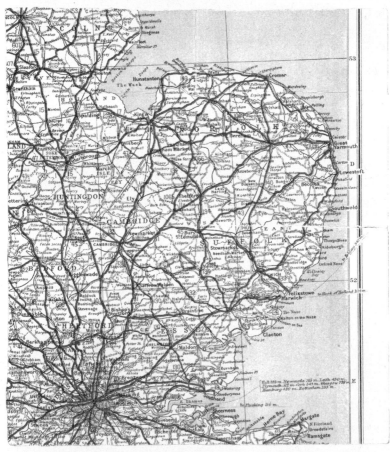

The map of East Anglia found on Karel Richter's person when searched at the police station he was taken to.

SPYDLE CHALLENGE

Unscramble the names of the following locations that Richter claimed to have visited, each of which is mentioned in the MI5 report and is also located within the region covered by the map opposite. Ignore the spaces and punctuation below when doing so.

Location Richter claimed to have just arrived from:

CP, I WISH (7)

Other locations Richter claimed to have visited:

CORR ME (6)

RICH NOW (7)

GRAB MEDIC (9)

STERN MUDDY BUS (4, 2, 7)

Can you also unscramble the country of Richter's birth, according to his passport? It has subsequently been divided into two modern countries.

VOCALIZE A SHOCK (14)

94: SKETCHY SURVEILLANCE

By the time of his arrest, it was thought that German spy
Karel Richter had been in the country for several days since his
parachute landing. The sketch below shows the approximate
locations of where some of Richter's possessions were found in
the area where he was captured.

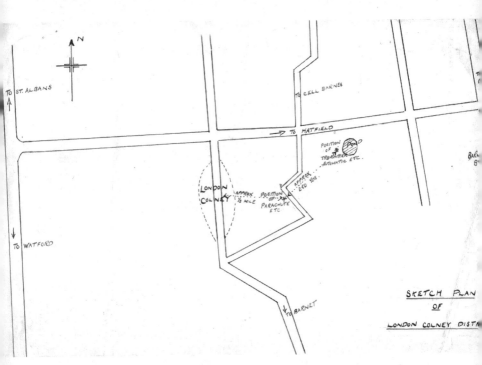

Secret Services's sketch of the area in which Karel Richter's parachute and wireless set
were located.

SPYDLE CHALLENGE

Imagine you are in charge of putting together the report on a recently discovered spy who has parachuted into the area. They have with them several items, which they have buried to help conceal their identity and mission. The items have been found in four different locations. Use the following information, along with the chart, to complete the table below showing which item was buried in which location, and in what order they were discovered:

- The wood was either the site of the second discovery, or where the map of targets was found – but not both
- The first discovery was either the codebook or was made in the haystack – but not both
- The transmitter was found in the wood
- The map of targets was found in the well
- The haystack was the third discovery

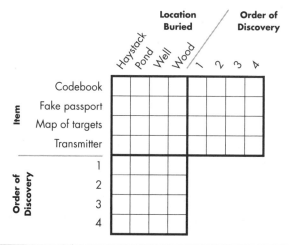

Item	Location Buried	Order of Discovery
		1
		2
		3
		4

95: KEEPING AN EYE OUT

Karel Richter's mission in England was to check on another
German agent who the Nazis suspected of having betrayed them
to become a double agent. Only when Richter was presented
to Josef Jakobs, another German agent who had already been
apprehended, did Richter begin to break and reveal the truth to
his interrogators.

Secret Service photos of some of Karel Richter's equipment.

SPYDLE CHALLENGE

Use your code-cracking skills to reveal the name of the agent – who was in fact a double agent – Richter had been sent to check up on. To do so, solve the crossword-style clues and write the resulting words into the numbered boxes. In these boxes each letter has been replaced by a number, with each number always representing the same letter. Once you have identified which letter is represented by every number, you can complete the final row of boxes to reveal the name.

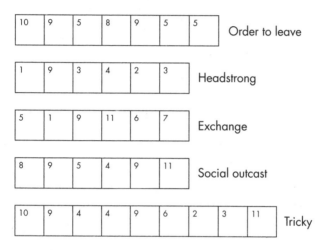

| 10 | 9 | 5 | 8 | 9 | 5 | 5 | Order to leave |

| 1 | 9 | 3 | 4 | 2 | 3 | Headstrong |

| 5 | 1 | 9 | 11 | 6 | 7 | Exchange |

| 8 | 9 | 5 | 4 | 9 | 11 | Social outcast |

| 10 | 9 | 4 | 4 | 9 | 6 | 2 | 3 | 11 | Tricky |

Name of double agent:

| 1 | 2 | 3 | 4 | | 5 | 6 | 7 | 8 | 9 | 10 | 11 |

You can use the grid below to keep track of your working out:

| 1 | 2 | 3 | 4 | 5 | 6 | 7 | 8 | 9 | 10 | 11 |

96: A VERY TALL TALE

Irwin Henry Richard Sanders was an intelligence nuisance, fantasist and fraudster who arrived in the UK in 1941 and was initially suspected of being a Nazi spy or sympathiser. During his internment he gave several different accounts of his background, parentage and provenance. Later he assumed different aliases and made fraudulent passport applications claiming to be British.

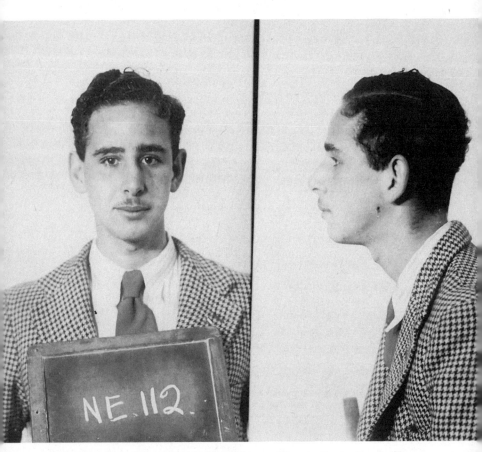

Photos of Dutchman Irwin Saunders, from Subjects of Security Service Enquiry files.

SPYDLE CHALLENGE

Imagine you have been tasked with unpicking the story of a suspected spy, who may or may not be an official intelligence nuisance designed to preoccupy your department. They have given you an account of their movements and activities in the last year, which span various cities in Europe. You need to understand the detail of their claims before you can attempt to verify them. You know that:

- They say they were recruited in Madrid at some point before they were deported from Rome
- They were injured in Lisbon immediately after being airlifted to Vienna
- The parachute drop into Budapest came immediately before being arrested in Gdansk
- They were recruited in Madrid after, but not immediately after, being imprisoned in Utrecht
- The injury in Lisbon came immediately prior to the imprisonment in Utrecht
- They were arrested in Gdansk immediately prior to being airlifted to Vienna
- After being trained in Paris they immediately escaped to Prague

In what order does the 'spy' claim that these events took place? Number each event with the order in which it took place:

Airlifted to Vienna	☐	Injured in Lisbon	☐
Arrested in Gdansk	☐	Parachuted into Budapest	☐
Deported from Rome	☐	Recruited in Madrid	☐
Escaped to Prague	☐	Trained in Paris	☐
Imprisoned in Utrecht	☐		

97: APPEARANCE IS EVERYTHING

László von Almásy was a Hungarian pilot and explorer who was recruited by the Abwehr, the German military intelligence, at the beginning of the Second World War. A heavily fictionalised version of his life story was later immortalised in the novel and film *The English Patient.*

PF ᵤᵤᵤ₂₀   According to C.S.D.I.C. this is an exact description of [ALMASSY.] MOHSEN FADL, on being shown a pre-war photograph of ALMASSY, stated that it was very like "MERAN", but that the latter was thinner. As ALMASSY is known to have "fined down" since the photo was taken, there is very little doubt that the two are identical.

Security Services report of positive identification of László von Almásy.

SPYDLE CHALLENGE

The document from which the fragment opposite is taken also contains a detailed physical description of Almásy, along with the languages he spoke. Some of the words used in the description have been given below, but those in upper case have been jumbled. Can you reveal the original descriptions?

Build: HINT

Hair: KARD NOBLED

Nose: AFT and UNUSEDLOP

Face: MALLS and HINT

Dressed: LASHIBBY

Gait: Walks with PIGDONOR shoulders

Languages: MANGER, CHEFRN and CRABAI

98: EXPEDITIOUS ENCOUNTERS

László von Almásy was involved in one of the most interesting failures of German espionage in Egypt, which largely contributed to 'breaking up the Egyptian fifth column': Operation Salam. In May 1942, Almásy was the head of an expedition to drive two German agents, Johannes Eppler and Heinrich Sandstede – known as Max and Moritz – across the desert from the Libyan oasis of Gialo to the Egyptian town of Asyut. (A 'fifth column' is an operation to undermine an enemy from within.)

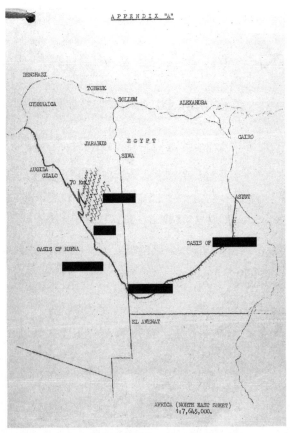

Sketch map of László von Almásy's route through the Libyan desert.

SPYDLE CHALLENGE

Use your powers of logic and deduction to reveal the locations, which have been concealed on the map opposite, and which were passed through on the expedition – that was eventually successful after two aborted attempts.

- GIALO and ASYUT were the start and end points of the journey, respectively.
- KEBABO came after, but not immediately after, the SAND DUNES
- DAKBLA KARGA was next on the route after GILF EL KEBIR
- KEBABO was visited between GILF EL KEBIR and the SAND DUNES, but not necessarily in that order

Number each location with the order in which it was visited:

ASYUT ☐

DAKBLA KARGA ☐

GIALO ☐

GILF EL KEBIR ☐

KEBABO ☐

SAND DUNES ☐

SIGHEN ☐

99: RETROSPECTIVE REPORT

While the two German agents, Eppler and Sandstede, were successfully delivered to Asyut, Egypt, the operation's success largely ended there. The agents were arrested after they encountered Viktor Hauer, a fellow German turned double agent for the British. Eppler was clearly displeased with his German colleagues, as is evident in the transcript below of the first conversation they had following their arrest.

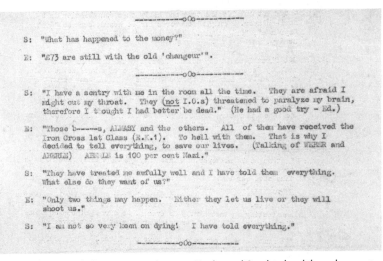

S: "What has happened to the money?"

E: "£73 are still with the old 'changeur'".

S: "I have a sentry with me in the room all the time. They are afraid I might cut my throat. They (not I.O.s) threatened to paralyze my brain, therefore I thought I had better be dead." (He had a good try - Ed.)

E: "Those b------s, ALMASY and the others. All of them have received the Iron Cross 1st Class (E.K.1). To hell with them. That is why I decided to tell everything, to save our lives. (Talking of WEBER and ABERLE) ABERLE is 100 per cent Nazi."

S: "They have treated me awfully well and I have told them everything. What else do they want of us?"

E: "Only two things may happen. Either they let us live or they will shoot us."

S: "I am not so very keen on dying! I have told everything."

Transcript of recorded conversation between Eppler and Sandstede while under arrest.

SPYDLE CHALLENGE

The text below is a documented quote from Eppler, after he and Sandstede had been apprehended. Use your code-cracking skills to reveal the encoded message in full, which relates to Almásy in some way. The message has been disguised with a Caesar shift, whereby each letter has been 'shifted' forwards a fixed number of positions through the alphabet. With a shift of +1, for example, A shifts to B, B to C and so on until Z shifts to A.

Work out what size of shift has been used to encode the below, to reveal what Eppler had to say about Almásy:

Ol O kbkx skkz Grsgye

gmgot, Muj, nuc O

yngrr hkgz nos av

100: AN EXPENSIVE MISSION

Josef Jakobs was a German intelligence service agent who was parachuted into Britain during the Second World War.

Found among Jakobs' possessions were a small radio for transmitting messages, a secret code wheel which he had torn into pieces, a number of forged documents – including an ID card in the name of James Rymer – and a considerable sum of cash.

NATIONAL REGISTRATION	NATIONAL REGISTRATION
656 301 29	656 301 29
James Rymer	James Rymer

1. This Identity Card must be carefully preserved. You may need it under conditions of national emergency for important purposes. You must not lose it or allow it to be stolen. If, nevertheless, it is stolen or completely lost, you must report the fact in person at any local National Registration Office.

2. You may have to show your Identity Card to persons who are authorised by law to ask you to produce it.

3. You must not allow your Identity Card to pass into the hands of unauthorised persons or strangers. Every grown up person should be responsible for the keeping of his or her Identity Card. The Identity Card of a child should be kept by the parent or guardian or person in charge of the child for the time being.

4. Anyone finding this Card must hand it in at a Police Station or National Registration Office.

DO NOTHING WITH THIS PART UNTIL YOU ARE TOLD

Full Postal Address of Above Person :—

London

33 Abbotsford Gdns

Woodford Green

(Signed) *James Rymer*.

Date 4th June 40

51-3120 2

Fake identity card used by German spy Josef Jakobs.

SPYDLE CHALLENGE

Use your mathematical skills to reveal the sum of money found along with Jakobs' other possessions. To calculate it, start with the number at the top-left of the chain, then follow the arrows to apply each operation in turn until you reach the 'TOTAL' box, writing your answer at the bottom. For the full Spydle challenge, try to do the entire calculation in your head without writing anything down until you reach the final TOTAL area.

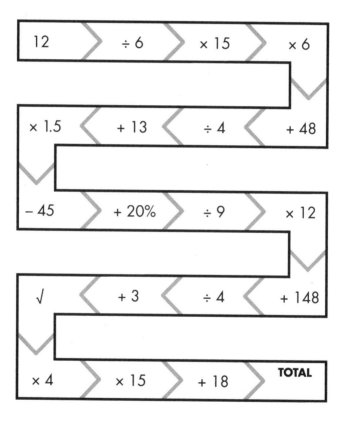

12	÷ 6	× 15	× 6
× 1.5	+ 13	÷ 4	+ 48
− 45	+ 20%	÷ 9	× 12
√	+ 3	÷ 4	+ 148
× 4	× 15	+ 18	**TOTAL**

How many pounds sterling was Jakobs found with?

101: WEATHERING THE STORM

MI5 interrogated the recently landed German spy Josef Jakobs, who appeared to have sustained serious injuries. After questioning, it was discovered that Jakobs had been sent to England to send back reports on weather conditions, possibly to record data for flying conditions.

Photograph of torch and battery found upon German spy Josef Jakobs.

SPYDLE CHALLENGE

Imagine you are looking through the possessions of a suspected spy, and come across an as-yet-incomplete report that they plan to send back to their contacts. You know that they have recorded the weather at four different locations, each on a different day and at a different time. Each time, a different weather condition was recorded. Here's what their notes say so far:

- Sunday's report was either in Hampstead or the day with clear skies – but not both
- The 7am report was either of drizzle or took place on Sunday – but not both

- The clear skies were noted on either Friday or Sunday
- Sunday's report was either taken at 4pm or said that it was overcast – but not both
- Richmond was not the site of the overcast report
- The 9pm recording did not take place in Greenwich
- On Sunday, either a hailstorm or drizzle was noted
- The Ilford report was of clear skies
- Monday's report did not take place in Richmond

Can you use these notes, along with the chart, to complete the report table below showing the conditions the spy observed on each day, and where and at what time?

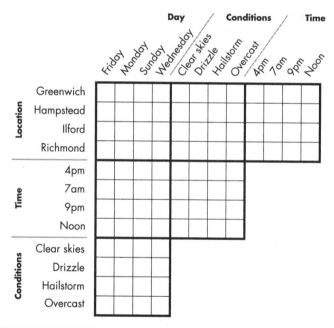

Location	Day	Time	Conditions

102: LAST ON THE LIST

Following intensive questioning, MI5 felt that they had gained all the useful intelligence that they could from Jakobs and had sufficient evidence for a trial. The transcript bears testimony to Jakobs' limited grasp of English and the result of the trial appears to have been something of a foregone conclusion. Jakobs was found guilty, and the only sentence open to the court was death.

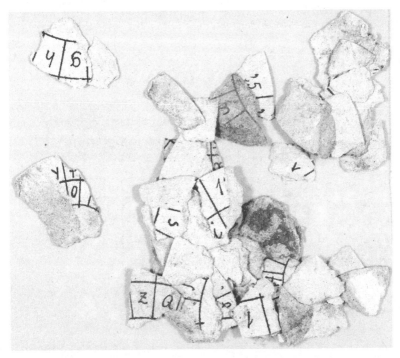

Photograph of the torn-up cipher used by Josef Jakobs to encrypt messages.

SPYDLE CHALLENGE

Use your codebreaking skills to determine the following details of Jakobs' life. The words in upper case have each been disguised with a Caesar shift, where each letter has been 'shifted' forwards a fixed number of positions. With a shift of +1, for example, A shifts to B, B to C and so on until Z shifts to A. The same shift has been used for all these words.

Country of birth: VEHOWLYEBQ

County of parachute landing: MKWLBSNQOCRSBO

City Jakobs was ordered to send reports from: VYXNYX

Hospital where he was sent for surgery: NEVGSMR

Place of execution: DYGOB YP VYXNYX

103: A DOUBLE DECOY

Operation Mincemeat was a plan by British military intelligence to mislead the Germans into thinking the Allies were about to invade Greece and Sardinia, prior to the actual invasion of Sicily. A fictional officer, Major William Martin, was created using the body of a deceased tramp who was dropped into the ocean and washed up on the coast of Spain, along with a briefcase containing false documents.

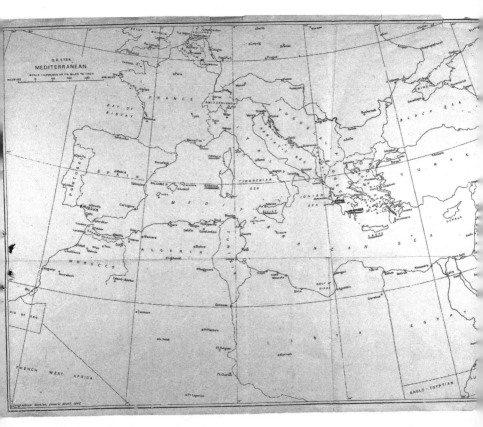

Map of Operation Mincemeat results.

SPYDLE CHALLENGE

Among the papers in the briefcase was a letter supposedly detailing an operation to invade Greece and the island of Sardinia, which had been given a codename. Use your linguistic and deductive skills to reveal the codename of the operation, which is a nine-letter word. Jumbled up in the target area circled below are the letters of the codename (which is also a regular English word), which can be formed using each letter exactly once.

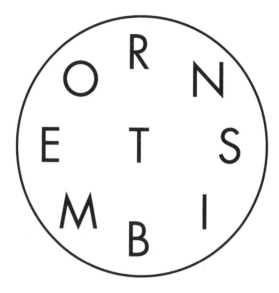

How many additional words can you form that use the centre letter plus two or more of the other letters? No letter may be used more times than it appears within the circle. There are over 120 more words to find, not including proper nouns.

104: THE MAN WHO NEVER WAS

The fictional officer, William Martin, was given a complex backstory with the use of the papers which were placed in the briefcase. The documents included a picture of an imaginary fiancée, along with several letters, ticket stubs, cash and a fake identification document.

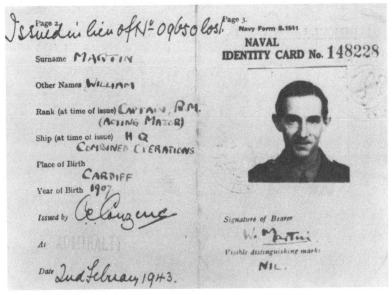

Operation Mincemeat identity card produced for the fictitious Major William Martin.

SPYDLE CHALLENGE

Imagine you are in charge of a secret decoy operation and need to create a body of evidence for a fictional individual, to give their story credibility. Use your strategy and planning skills to complete your to-do list for your mission by working out what order to complete the eight tasks in. You know that it must be the case that:

- You need to buy cinema tickets immediately after acquiring a false uniform
- You need to forge letters immediately after creating a fake ID card
- You will buy cinema tickets at some point after inventing a family tree
- Creating a fake ID card is the first item
- Buying cinema tickets will take place between taking a photo of their 'wife' and inventing a family tree, although not necessarily in that order
- Packing their briefcase is the last item
- Cutting a bunch of keys will come immediately after buying cinema tickets

Number each to-do list item with the order in which it must be done:

Acquire false uniform ☐   Forge letters ☐

Buy cinema tickets ☐   Invent family tree ☐

Create fake ID card ☐   Pack briefcase ☐

Cut bunch of keys ☐   Take photo of 'wife' ☐

105: IMPERSONAL EFFECTS

As part of Operation Mincemeat, false 'pocket litter' was created and placed on Major Martin's body to convince the Germans of the authenticity of his identity. A record was kept of the items that accompanied the body as well as a report of the clothing Martin was dressed in.

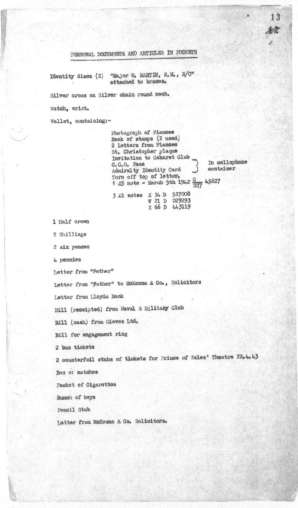

Operation Mincemeat detailed list of personal documents and articles on Major Martin's person.

SPYDLE CHALLENGE

Fit each of the words listed below into the grid, one letter per box, so each reads from left to right or top to bottom. Ignore any spaces. Once complete, the highlighted letters can be rearranged to spell out the surname of Martin's supposed superior officer, who was the sender of some of the fake letters in Martin's briefcase.

3-letter word
TIE

4-letter words
BILL
COAT
KEYS
PASS
VEST

5-letter words
BOOTS
GLOVE
PANTS
SHIRT
SOCKS

6-letter words
BLOUSE
BRACES
ID CARD
PENCIL
STAMPS
TICKET

7-letter words
GAITERS
LETTERS
MATCHES
PENNIES
RECEIPT

8-letter word
TROUSERS

106: AN UNCANNY LIKENESS

Operation Copperhead was a small military deception operation run by the British during the Second World War. It formed part of Operation Bodyguard, the cover plan for the invasion of Normandy in 1944, and was intended to mislead German intelligence as to the location of General Bernard Montgomery.

The German high command expected Montgomery (one of the best-known Allied commanders) to play a key role in any cross-channel bridgehead. A high-profile appearance outside the United Kingdom would suggest that an Allied invasion was not imminent. An appropriate lookalike was found: M. E. Clifton James, who spent a short time with Montgomery to familiarise himself with the general's mannerisms. On 26 May 1944, James flew first to Gibraltar and then to Algiers, making appearances where the Allies knew German intelligence agents would spot him. He then remained in hiding until Montgomery's public appearance in Normandy following the invasion.

Press clipping from the Daily Express of the Operation Copperhead plan, dated October 1945.

SPYDLE CHALLENGE

The eight words listed below *should* form a coherent set, but they are not as they appear since exactly one letter has been changed in each word in order to disguise them. Use your language and deductive skills to change exactly one letter in each word so that they all form a linked set. As a clue, the first item in that set is linked to Operation Copperhead in some way.

CAIRN

LION

RIGS

NINE

PLAGUE

PARTS

SIENNA

MAPLES

107: POTENTIAL PROJECTS

During the course of the war, several codenames were proposed for potential use during covert operations of both large and small scale.

Cabinet Office record of report to the Prime Minister indicating the widespread use of codenames.

SPYDLE CHALLENGE

Fit all but one of these historical proposed codenames on the list into the grid, one letter per box, so they each read either across or down. The leftover name that will not fit with the others is the codename given to joint SOE and OSS (UK and US intelligence services) operations undertaken in the Adriatic region.

5-letter words
BRICK
CONGO
FLOOD
PARRY
RALLY
SUPER

6-letter words
ACTION
CLUTCH
FRENZY

HOTPOT
IMPISH
JAGGED
KLAXON
LAUNCH
LEADER
MAROON
SLEUTH
THRUST
THWART
URGENT

7-letter words
FORTUNE
GRAPPLE
LIGHTER
MARINER
SALIENT
SOLDIER
SUNBEAM

8-letter words
RESOLUTE
REVOLVER
THROTTLE
VEHEMENT

9-letter words
SOVEREIGN
STEADFAST

108: FRIENDLY FACT-FINDING

BRIXMIS was the British Commanders'-in-Chief Mission to the Soviet Forces in Germany. It was set up in 1946 to facilitate military liaison and good working relations between the Western Allies and the Soviets.

Its main purpose was to monitor the deployment and capability of Warsaw Pact forces. Freedom of travel was allowed, in marked vehicles, to the various missions in each other's zones, with the exception of restricted sites. This presented the ideal opportunity for intelligence gathering for both sides. These incursions turned into a game of cat and mouse, with BRIXMIS tours trailed and harassed by the East German authorities.

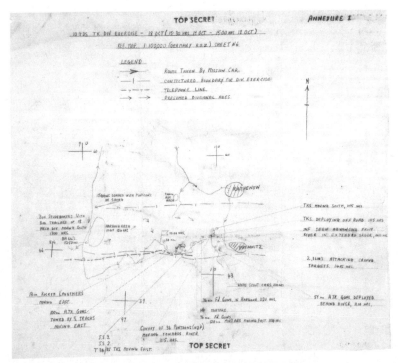

Route map of the 10 Guards Tank Division exercise on 18 October 1951.

SPYDLE CHALLENGE

Imagine you are an intelligence officer putting together a covert report on the movements of foreign forces. You have received information about the unexpected activities of eight supposedly reserve units – codenamed A to H – and want to work out in what order they were mobilised. You also know that:

- H was mobilised immediately after A, and immediately before G
- E was the first to be mobilised, while D was last
- H was mobilised later than C
- B was mobilised before, but not immediately before, C

Number each unit with the order in which it was mobilised:

A ☐   E ☐

B ☐   F ☐

C ☐   G ☐

D ☐   H ☐

109: JUST KEEPING TABS

BRIXMIS lasted until just before the reunification of Germany in 1990. Each liaison mission could involve up to 31 people, consisting of no more than 11 officers. They were expected to remain in recognisable uniform, and travel in clearly identifiable vehicles.

9. JESERIG - T-54. 16 FEB 67

Photo of a Soviet Army T-54 tank in Jeserig, East Germany, from a BRIXMIS Quarterly Report.

SPYDLE CHALLENGE

Imagine you are putting together a report following a tour which included some surreptitious intelligence gathering. You spotted four different types of vehicle convoys being moved in four different directions out of the city, at four different times of day. The number of vehicles, in each case, was different. Complete a full report by filling in the table below, based on the chart and the following observations:

- The vehicles moving north were not spotted at 2pm
- The 12pm observation was of tanks
- The vehicles moving south were trailers
- The trailers were not in a group of eight
- The trains were not seen in the east
- There were 15 vehicles seen heading north
- The pontoons were not seen at 7am
- Either the trains were seen at 10am, or there were four of them
- The group of 15 vehicles were either pontoons or trailers
- The 2pm vehicle sighting did not reveal them heading west

	Direction of Travel				Time of Day				Vehicle Count			
	East	North	South	West	7am	10am	12pm	2pm	4	8	12	15
Pontoon												
Tank												
Trailer												
Train												
4												
8												
12												
15												
7am												
10am												
12pm												
2pm												

Vehicle Type	Direction of Travel	Vehicle Count	Time of Day

110: THE BRIDGE OF SPIES

The Bridge of Spies is the alternative name given to Glienicke Bridge near Potsdam, just to the south-west of Berlin, as it was the site of several exchanges of captured spies during the Cold War. Its location on the border between West Berlin and East Germany made it a convenient spot for these exchanges to take place. In 1962 this was where the Soviet spy Rudolph Abel was swapped for Gary Powers, the American U2 pilot shot down over the Soviet Union in 1960.

The image below depicts a handover in 1975.

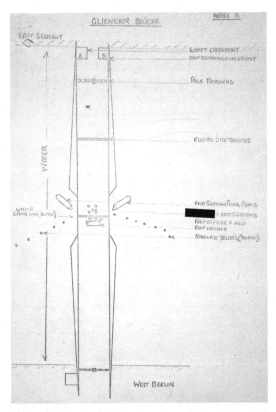

Sketch plan of the Glienicke Bridge used in exchanges of captured spies.

SPYDLE CHALLENGE

Imagine you are an agent whose cover has been blown, and you need to evacuate a city full of bridges by the most direct route you can. Find your way from the top of the maze-like map below all the way to the bottom, as quickly as you can. Some paths pass under or over other paths using the given bridges.

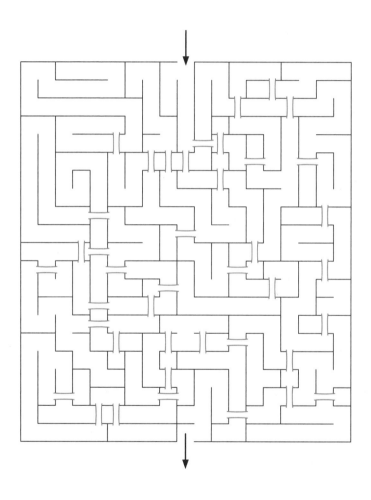

6 CODES, CIPHERS AND GADGETS

Codes and ciphers have been used to carry secret messages in times of war and unrest, protecting military and political information should messages fall into the hands of the enemy. Codes use groups of letters, numbers or symbols to replace complete words and phrases. Generally, a codebook is used to send or receive a coded message. Ciphers use letters, numbers or symbols to replace individual letters and numbers, and a key is used to encipher and decipher messages.

During the Second World War, German officials and military forces used an innovative electro-mechanical device known as the Enigma machine to protect their top-secret radio traffic. Throughout the war a team of British and Polish mathematicians and cryptanalysts were based at Bletchley Park (codenamed Station X), working around the clock to unscramble the streams of intercepted information. Enigma created a new form of encryption based on mathematics, not language. An understanding of letter frequency and linguistic patterns would not crack Enigma encoded messages. The capture of an Enigma machine and codebooks from a German U-boat on 9 May 1941 and other more conventional acts of espionage led to significant breakthroughs. The National Archives declassified these records in the 1970s, enabling the story of the breaking of the Enigma cipher to be one of the most celebrated of the war.

Sabotage and subversion during the Second World War was largely undertaken by agents operating abroad, and recruits came from Britain and across occupied Europe. The Special Operations Executive (SOE) issued a sabotage handbook to agents to ensure that operations caused maximum disruption. Sabotage operations required the use of ingenious devices such as explosives and booby traps. These were manufactured in Britain and were disguised in many ways. They were inspected in specially requisitioned rooms in the Natural History Museum before being issued to agents. German agents also operated in Britain, and they too had their own gadgets and devices which, when confiscated, were examined by the scientists and technicians who were employed at research facilities. The examples in this chapter illustrate just some of the specialist equipment used by agents on both sides.

111: SUFFRAGETTE CODE

The suffragette movement at the turn of the century became problematic for the Home Office. Fighting for the right to vote, two passionate and active suffragettes, Hilda Burkitt (whose alias was 'Byron') and Florence Tunks, became involved in many illegal activities. The police began to closely monitor them following Byron's attempt to burn down Leeds Football Ground, which resulted in a short term in prison. Undeterred by imprisonment, they both hatched a plan to burn down the newly renovated Bath Hotel in Felixstowe. At the time of their arrest, the police found in their possession a coded diary that proved their guilt. They were convicted of arson and imprisoned in Holloway Prison for women.

Bath Hotel, Felixstowe, burned down in suffragette protest April 1914.

List of coded entries in Byron's diary held in her Home Office file.

SPYDLE CHALLENGE

According to a police report, several coded entries in Byron's diary were thought to indicate that she had undertaken successful – or unsuccessful – 'outrages' on a particular day. An entry with 'NO GO', for example, would indicate a day with no success.

Use your tracking skills to discover eight entries from Byron's diary that were thought by the police to indicate 'successful outrages'. To do so, start on the top-left square below and find a path that visits every grid square. As it travels, the path must spell out each of the eight entries in turn, some of which consist of multiple words. The path can only travel horizontally or vertically between squares, and will finish at the bottom-right square.

B	A	L	A	T	S	U	C	C
A	D	L	E	R	A	S	S	E
N	W	H	I	G	L	I	T	T
C	E	T	S	E	E	D	E	L
I	R	D	P	P	R	A	H	T
V	E	H	I	O	I	Y	G	G
I	C	O	R	D	O	L	I	A
N	E	M	L	L	S	E	C	M
D	E	R	E	A	D	A	N	E

Use the blank spaces below to write in the entries as you come across them, writing one letter per underline:

1. _ _ _ _

2. _ _ _ _ _

3. _ _ _ _ _   _ _ _ _ _

4. _ _ _ _ _ _ _ _ _ _

5. _ _ _ _ _ _ _ _ _ _   _ _ _ _ _

6. _ _ _ _ _ _

7. _ _ _ _ _   _ _ _ _ _ _ _

8. _   _ _ _ _ _ _   _ _ _ _ _ _ _ _ _   _ _ _ _

112: DEFT DEFINITION

During the Second World War a brochure providing guidance of overseas postal censorship was published by the War Office. The code section of the brochure describes various visual ways to conceal hidden meanings. Below is an illustrated fashion plate from the brochure in which a system of Morse (not the usual dots and dashes) has been introduced into the embroidery of dresses.

The coded message in figures 1 to 3 is 'Heavy reinforcements for the enemy expected hourly'.

SPYDLE CHALLENGE

The following text is taken directly from the first pages of the postal censorship guide. Some of the words in this paragraph, however, have been encoded with a Caesar cipher to conceal the passage's full meaning. Each letter in the upper-cased words has been 'shifted' forwards a fixed number of positions. With a shift of +1, for example, A shifts to B, B to C and so on until Z shifts to A. All of the words use the same shift.
Can you use your code-cracking skills to reveal the words in upper case and reveal the passage as it appears in the guide?

'What is Code? Several LMNQVQBQWVA have been used to LMAKZQJM Code. It has been AXWSMV of as a LQAOCQAM; as a UMBPWL of KTWBPQVO words and AMVBMVKMA so that only those with AXMKQIT SVWETMLOM can AMM through the LQAOCQAM; as the KTWISQVO of QVNWZUIBQWV so that only the QVQBQIBML can XQMZKM the DMQT.'

113: SIGNED, SEALED, DECIPHERED

Prisoner-of-war mail was subject to postal censorship by both the military and civil postal service. Examples of the various methods used during the Second World War were recorded by the Ministry of Defence. One example below shows positions, values and placements of postal stamps on envelopes to communicate information based on an agreed code.

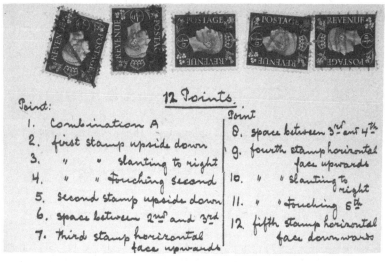

Stamp codes from the Postal and Telegraph Censorship Department.

SPYDLE CHALLENGE

Imagine you are responsible for deciphering a potential code that uses postage stamps, and are close to cracking it. You believe that there are three possible messages being conveyed between agents, with different combinations of stamp value and stamp placement on letters. You want to know what each particular arrangement of a stamp's value and angle means, as well as whether it is touching another stamp. Use the chart and notes below to complete the table:

- None of the messages involved a 2d stamp that was the right way up
- The message about troops being on the move did not involve a ½d stamp
- Cover blown can be communicated using 2d stamps
- A ½d stamp should be placed sideways
- Troops on the move is communicated by making sure a stamp either touches one other stamp or is upside down – but not both
- The code involving touching two stamps did not involve 2d stamps

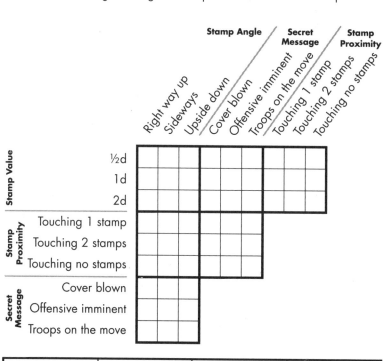

Stamp value	Stamp Angle	Stamp Proximity	Secret Message

114: PORTUGUESE PARAPHRASING

Some codes involved substituting military or sensitive vocabulary with seemingly innocent, household words. The note below gives details of a 'plain language' code that uses Portuguese. For example, the name of the aircraft 'Boston Bomber' was substituted with the word 'Madeira'.

<u>TRANSLATION</u>

4760

The strength of the military forces will be denoted by the word TONELADA (Ton). Each ton represents 1,000 men; 10,000 men - 10 tons, 5,000 men - 5 tons, half a ton - 500 men.

Guns will be denoted by the word QUILO (Kilo), each 200k. represents one piece, i.e. 18 guns - 3,600k.

Anti-aircraft guns will be denoted by the words METROS DE FASENDA (Metres of material), each metre represents one piece or each 4 metres one battery, i.e. 3 anti-aircraft guns - 3 metres of material; 4 batteries - 12 metres of material.

Machine-guns will be denoted by the word GARRAFA (bottle), each bottle represents a machine-gun. i.e. 8 machine-guns - 8 bottles.

Aeroplanes will be denoted by the words TUBOS (pipes) and FRASCOS (flagons); each pipe, a bomber and each flagon a fighter, i.e. 50 fighters and 20 bombers - 50 flagons and 20 pipes. Transport planes will be denoted by the words GRANDES TUBOS (big pipes) and reconnaissance planes by the word GRANDES (big ones).

The following words will be denoted by a word which ends with these suffixes:-

Fortifications still under construction	ardo ardos
Fortifications built	aixa aixo
	aixas
	iga
North West	ar
South West	
Northern	
From the North of	esse
To the North	
Meridional	
From the South of	encia
To the South	

Translation note of a plain language code in Secret Service files.

SPYDLE CHALLENGE

Place each of these upper-case words into the grid below, one letter per box, so they read across from left to right on each row. Ignore any spaces, and the non-upper case 'Flying'. Some boxes span multiple lines, indicating letters in common between lines. Once complete, each militarily sensitive English word will line up with the Portuguese word which was used to disguise it.

ADMIRAL	Flying FORTRESS	OLD MODEL
AERODROMES	GENERAL	RECENT MODEL
COLONEL	HURRICANE	SPITFIRE
FACTORIES	MARTIN	

azeitonas (olives)

milho (maize)

trigo (corn)

azeite (oil)

pimenta (pepper)

remessa (remittance)

Portuguese escudos

encargo (charge, duty)

branco/velho (white/old)

preto/novo (black/new)

Angolares

115: NUMEROUS DISGUISES

Plain language codes and steganographic techniques were
used by German agents and others in the Second World War.
The memorandum below was attached to a file containing
instructions to censors for detecting these codes.

INTERNAL MEMORANDUM. 53a 943

From.....B.1.G.....Mr. Brooman-White,   To..B.3.D.....Mr..Grogan.............

> I attach some information about codes to be used by
> the▆▆▆ agent ▆▆▆ who is at present operating from
> Washington. As this man was recruited almost the same time
> as ▆▆, this information may well point the key to the latter
> case as well. It has unfortunately been buried in an S.I.S.
> file since last November. Will you please pass on the
> relevant information to Foyer?

Date 27.4.43.   Signature... R. Brooman-White

8. Form 161/B.P./20000/2.43.

Secret Service internal memorandum regarding detection of codes.

SPYDLE CHALLENGE

The 'attached codes' that are referenced in the memorandum opposite were predominantly used with Spanish-language text. One of these codes is a letter-to-number substitution cipher, whereby each letter is replaced by a number based on its relative position in the alphabet. In such a cipher, A may be replaced with 1, B with 2 and so on until Z is replaced with 26. In the Spanish example, A was replaced with 15, B with 16, and so on.

Use your code-cracking skills to reveal a quote relating to espionage attributed to the Duke of Marlborough in the 1700s. Each letter is replaced by a number, but it's up to you to work out which letter 'A' has been replaced with, and then crack the rest of the code from there.

19 20   28 6 23

8 6 19   7 10

8 20 19 9 26 8 25 10 9

24 26 8 8 10 24 24 11 26 17 17 30

28 14 25 13 20 26 25

10 6 23 17 30   6 19 9

12 20 20 9

14 19 25 10 17 17 14 12 10 19 8 10

116: COVERT CODES

Many military personnel set up personal coding systems with their families and friends for use in the event of capture. Under the Geneva Convention, prisoners of war were allowed to send and receive letters and so some used their own made-up codes to ask for specific items to be sent for use within the camps to aid escape. Some coded messages contained secret information for the intelligence services. These were often checked by the military and civil postal censors.

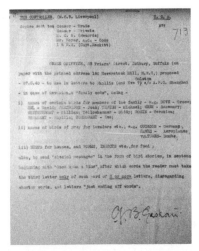

Example of a privately set up code from the Controllers Office.

SPYDLE CHALLENGE

Imagine you are trying to decipher a private code, discovered in correspondence between members of a family. They have given each other different, flower-related codenames, and are each in a different city. You want to understand which codename refers to which family member, relative to the sender of the letter you are currently trying to decode. Use the following information and chart to complete the table below:

- Paris is either where the cousin is located, or where Eugenia is – but not both
- The father is not Eugenia
- Neither Tokyo nor Melbourne are the location for BUSH
- Sarah is either the aunt or is in Paris, but not both
- BERRY is not in Tokyo
- Eugenia is either codenamed BRACKEN or is in Washington DC, but not both
- Sarah is either known as BLOSSOM or is the father, but not both
- BLOSSOM is in Washington DC
- Clive is not in Paris

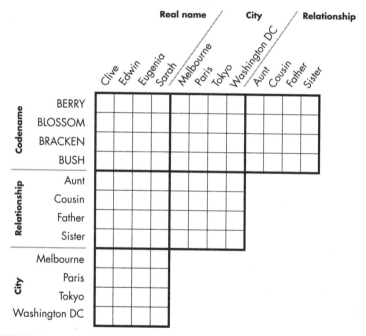

Codename	Real name	Relationship	City

117: MIXED MEANINGS

Military Intelligence 12 (MI12) liaised with the Code Section of the Censorship and Postal Office who often made suggestions on the type of code system being used.

To   : MAJOR BATCHELOR. M.I.12. P.W.

From   : CODE SECTION

Ref I.S.9/P/1121/736

Lieut. John A. Bull

We think the words on these cards are an anagram.

It is noticed that, with the exception of MAY and PEST, the remaining words are the same on both cards and these words should be capable of forming an anagram independently.

The solution in our view, is:-

1) MAY and PEST = MAY and SEPT.
2) ~~LEAD~~ ~~ANTIMONY~~.
   EMILY NOAT AND = LEAD ANTIMONY
   Both these minerals are mined in Siam and as the P/W has struck out both:

I am working for pay
and
I am not working

the implication is that he is on forced labour (unpaid) in the Lead and Antimony mines, and the two dates may cover the period from May to September, or, if the cards were posted at different dates, it would show that at both times of posting, he was engaged on the same work.

5th May 1944.

Note from Code Section indicating how a code can be deciphered.

SPYDLE CHALLENGE

Use your code-cracking and linguistic skills to unscramble the anagrammed words below, which are all connected in some way. One additional letter has been added to each anagram, however, which must be extracted. These extra letters, when read in order from top to bottom, spell out the theme linking the words. As a clue, all of the words might be found on a map. Ignore any spaces.

BUTH

LOUTEH

FAIRY COT

HUESOL

EMUS MUD

A SPOILT HI

NO LOCHS

BIG CAN

118: THE RIGHT MESSAGE

This rare message is very likely from a Second World War civilian internee in Thailand and probably has a hidden code. It has been carefully disguised on the back of what appears to be another piece of paper so as not to attract the attention of the Japanese authorities. The author appears to have fled Changi in Singapore for Thailand. It's unclear how much of the letter is truth or code.

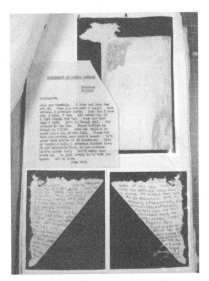

Photographs of a secret message from an internee in Thailand and its transcription.

SPYDLE CHALLENGE

Imagine you are in charge of intercepting post, to redact sensitive information and look for secret codes in correspondence. You have identified four personal letters which you believe in fact each contain a different secret code, with each posted from and to a different city. In addition, each letter also contains a different name that needs to be redacted. Summarise this information by completing the table at the bottom of the page, based on the chart and the following notes:

- The mail from Cape Town is either en route to Buenos Aires or needs 'Monty' redacted – but not both
- The letter from which 'Blondie' must be removed originated from London
- The number code is not heading to Oslo
- The letter which needs 'Monty' redacted is either from Amsterdam or from London
- The Caesar cipher letter refers to 'Reggie', which must be redacted, although it is not on the way to Oslo
- The underlined letters are used in either the letter to Buenos Aires or the letter to Moscow
- Cairo is not the destination of the London letter
- 'Blondie' must be redacted from either the number code letter or the one going to Buenos Aires – but not both

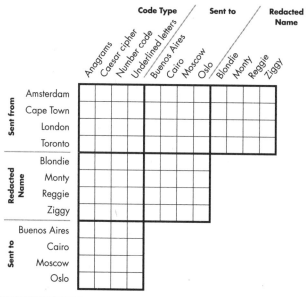

Sent from	Code Type	Redacted Name	Sent to

119: CRACKING STUFF

The Enigma machine was used by the German military during the Second World War to send secure messages. The code was strengthened at the start of the war through daily changes to the cipher. The code was thought by the German armed forces to be unbreakable.

Photograph of the Enigma machine from records of the Government Code and Cypher School (GCCS).

SPYDLE CHALLENGE

Use your code-cracking skills to reveal the names of several cities, uncovering a pattern of encryption to help you predict the next code. The names of English cities below have all been encoded with a Caesar shift, where each letter has been 'shifted' forwards a fixed number of positions. With a shift of 1, for example, A shifts to B, B to C and so on until Z shifts to A.

Each name has been encoded with a different shift, and the pattern of shift numbers forms a sequence when read from top to bottom. Write down the size of each shift and discern the sequence to help you decode the full set of words.

NBODIFTUFS
Shift size: ____

DNCEMRQQN
Shift size: ____

RIAGEWXPI
Shift size: ____

IPYTPUNOHT
Shift size: ____

WZYOZY
Shift size: ____

BUUTI
Shift size: ____

120: DEUS EX MACHINA

Alan Turing and fellow codebreaker Gordon Welchman
invented the Bombe, a machine that deciphered the Enigma
codes and enabled a vast quantity of top-secret German military
correspondence to be read. The intelligence it provided was
particularly pivotal during the Battle of the Atlantic.

An Enigma intercept, dated August 1944.

SPYDLE CHALLENGE

Imagine that you have been able to decrypt enemy transmissions and have discovered fragments of a set of plans related to several planned naval attacks. You realise that there are four planned attacks, each to take place in a different sea area and with a different codename. Different numbers of enemy vessels are due to carry out each attack, using convoy techniques. You also know that:

- The attack codename STRIFE involves 7 vessels
- The 4-vessel attack is not DART
- Bailey is where DODGE is due to take place
- The attack in Rockall does not involve 7 vessels
- The 2-vessel attack is either in sea area Bailey or codenamed STRIFE, but not both
- Shannon is the planned site of the 6-vessel attack

Which codenamed attack is due to occur in which area, and involving what number of vessels?

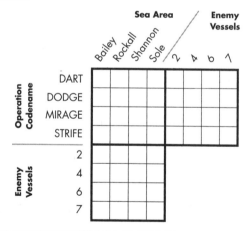

Operation Codename	Sea Area	Number of Vessels

121: A NEW SYSTEM

The Germans had used the Enigma machine for some time, and the Allies knew how to decode messages enciphered by it. At the start of the war, however, the Germans began to change the cipher daily, which made the task considerably more difficult.

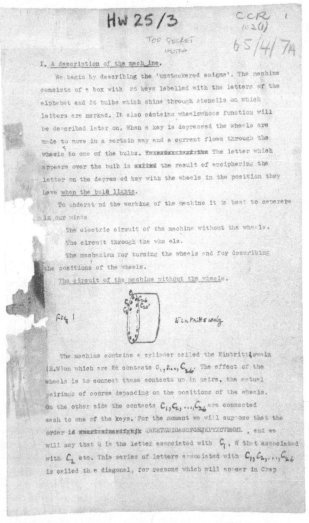

'Mathematical Theory of ENIGMA Machine' by Alan Turing, also known as 'Prof's book'.

SPYDLE CHALLENGE

Use your code-cracking skills to reveal the name of the cryptanalysis technique developed by Turing that allowed for the cracking of the Enigma code. To do so, solve the crossword-style clues and write the resulting words into the numbered boxes. In these boxes each letter has been replaced by a number, with each number always representing the same letter. Once you have identified which letter is represented by every number, you can complete the final row of boxes to reveal the name of the technique.

7	4	5	7	4	5

Mutter quietly

2	6	5	7	2	3

RAF flyer, perhaps

1	5	2	6	3	8

Thinking organs

7	6	3	6	7	4	7

Lowest amount

1	2	5	1	2	5	6	2	3

Savage

Name of Turing's cryptanalysis technique:

1	2	3	1	4	5	6	8	7	4	8

You can use the grid below to keep track of your working out:

1	2	3	4	5	6	7	8

122: A SHORTER WAR

The application of the vital intelligence obtained for the Allies by cracking the Enigma machine is thought to have shortened the war substantially.

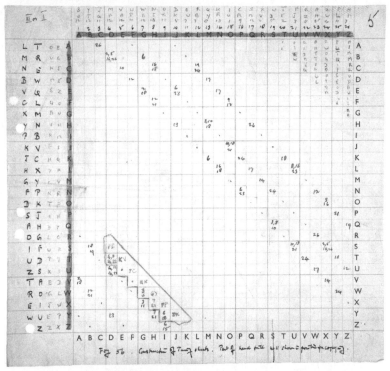

Calculations from Turing's paper 'Mathematical Theory of ENIGMA Machine'.

SPYDLE CHALLENGE

Use your numerical skills to reveal how many months the war is believed to have been shortened by, thanks to the cracking of the Enigma code. To calculate it, start with the number at the top of the chain, then follow the arrows to apply each operation in turn until you reach the 'TOTAL' box, writing your answer at the bottom. For the full Spydle challenge, try to do the entire calculation in your head without writing anything down until you reach the final TOTAL area.

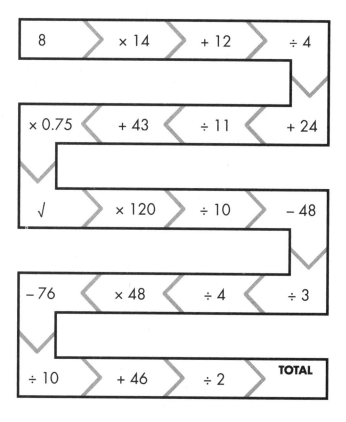

By how many months is the war believed to have been shortened?

123: HIGH PRAISE

Churchill's interest in military intelligence began during the First World War when he was First Lord of the Admiralty. A year after the outbreak of the Second World War he asked to be sent a copy of all decoded Enigma-encrypted messages from Bletchley Park every day. By 1941 this codebreaking establishment was short-staffed and a memo signed by Alan Turing prompted Churchill to visit the codebreakers to offer up his appreciation of their work and boost morale.

MOST SECRET.

10, Downing Street,
Whitehall.

September 27, 1940.

In confirmation of my telephone message, I have been personally directed by the Prime Minister to inform you that he wishes you to send him daily all the ENIGMA messages.

These are to be sent in a locked box with a clear notice stuck to it "THIS BOX IS ONLY TO BE OPENED BY THE PRIME MINISTER IN PERSON".

After seeing the messages he will return them to you.

Yours ever,

P.S. As there will be no check possible here, would you please institute a check on receipt of returned documents to see that you have got them all back.

C.

Request from No. 10 for Churchill to receive all the Enigma messages.

SPYDLE CHALLENGE

Use your tracking skills to reveal a description of the staff at Bletchley Park, alleged to have been made by Winston Churchill, which is based on a well-known expression. Starting on the grey square below, find a path that visits every grid square. As it travels, the path must spell out the expression, which is ten words long. The path can only travel horizontally or vertically between squares, and will finish next to the black square.

	T	H	E	E
H	T	E	G	S
E	D	L	O	E
G	I	A	H	W
O	E	N	E	G
L	D	E	N	G
A	C	V	D	S
C	R	E	N	A
K	L	E	D	

124: THE PEN IS MIGHTIER

Arthur Graham Owens was an Allied double agent during the Second World War and was known to MI5 as Agent Snow – with Snow derived from the letters of his surname, minus the central 'e'. MI5 did not trust him, and he was arrested in 1941 carrying the explosive pen and pencil shown below.

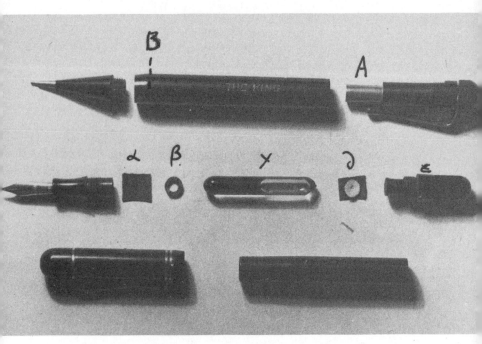

Photograph of Agent Snow's dismantled pencil and fountain pen. 'A' shown is the pencil's detonator.

SPYDLE CHALLENGE

Listed below are several household items which could have been used to hide explosive devices. Unfortunately, they have detonated prematurely, fracturing into several parts. Piece the fragments back together to reveal seven seemingly innocuous items, making sure that you use each fragment exactly once. Four of the items consist of two words, although the fragments do not include the space between words, while the remainder are each one word long.

AP	AST	ATE	BE
CH	CHO	COL	DER
EBOT	ELT	ETU	HERB
LEAT	OW	SO	TALC
THP	TLE	TOO	TOR
	UMP	WIN	

125: UNFORESEEN DELAY

The image below provides a visual breakdown of the structure of a German sabotage device which could be used to create delayed explosions, known as a '21-day time clock'.

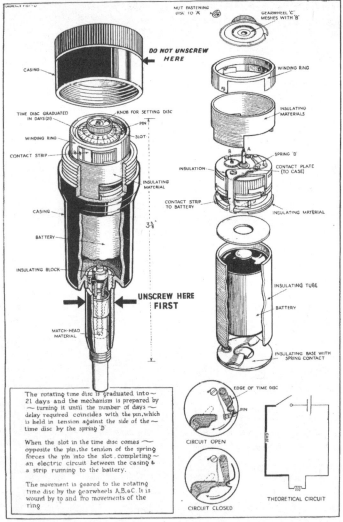

FIG. 7. Diagram of 21-day German time clock.

Diagram found in a report on the work of B1C, the counter-sabotage section of MI5.

SPYDLE CHALLENGE

Imagine you have discovered a series of explosive sabotage devices, each of which has been set to go off at a different time by a different codenamed spy. You want to work out the order in which each spy's device is due to detonate. You also know that:

- ASH placed the device due to detonate first
- NIMBUS's will detonate before MAPLE's
- The device planted by CUCKOO will detonate immediately before that planted by TROUT
- FROST's device will explode immediately before CUCKOO's
- The explosion caused by FOSS will be immediately before that caused by NIMBUS
- TROUT's explosion will come immediately before MAPLE's
- The spy codenamed NIMBUS planted a device that would explode at some time later than GRIZZLY's

Number each codename below with the order in which their device is due to detonate:

ASH ☐   GRIZZLY ☐

CUCKOO ☐   MAPLE ☐

FOSS ☐   NIMBUS ☐

FROST ☐   TROUT ☐

126: FALSE BOTTOMS

MI5's counter-sabotage intelligence helped discover the ingenious ways the German intelligence services were hiding explosive materials in objects such as this mess tin, typically used by Spanish dockyard workers at the base in Gibraltar. Featuring a false bottom, explosive elements could then be covered with real food to further conceal the explosives hidden beneath.

An explosive device disguised in a mess tin.

SPYDLE CHALLENGE

Imagine you are investigating the smuggling of explosive devices, and have found three mess tins with false bottoms. They each are disguised by containing a different genuine food, and each contain a different device.

Each is also destined for a different European city, and was found in the possession of a different codenamed individual. Combine the information below with the chart to fill in the table beneath:

- The primer is either heading to Bordeaux or hidden under the pie – but not both
- The primer is being carried by the person codenamed CLERK
- AJAX is not the codename of the person carrying the pie
- The tin en route to Bordeaux conceals the primer
- Madrid is either the destination of AJAX or where the mash is going – but not both
- The detonator is not hidden with the pie

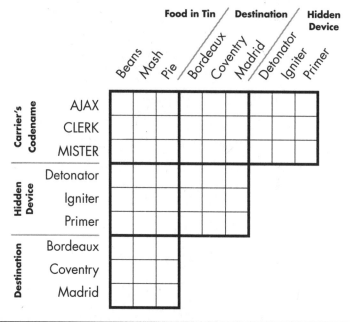

Carrier's Codename	Food in Tin	Hidden Device	Destination

127: NOT SO SWEET

The image below appears to be a box of Vichy pastilles – French-made sweets – but is in fact a disguised box of incendiaries.

A page from a catalogue of concealment devices used by German sabotage agents during the Second World War.

SPYDLE CHALLENGE

The names of ten items of confectionery are given below. Each name, however, is secretly hiding a weapon. Remove the name of the sweet from each line, to reveal the hidden weapon. Although they are mixed together, the letters in each word remain in correct reading order – and none are left unused. For example, '**PMASITINLELE**' is a 'PASTILLE' that conceals a 'MINE'.

SMWIONRTD

BRIOFNLBOEN

PGUIMSTDOROLP

TONROUPGEADTO

CRAORCAKMELET

MLIOSLSLIPOIPLE

CLAONZNENGOEN

SDHAEGRGBETER

BUCATTETRASPCUOLTCTH

MHUSUMKBEUTG

128: A CURIOUS CASE

This picture shows the interior of Agent Zigzag's (see puzzle 73) booby-trapped attaché case. An explosive is set to detonate once the case is opened.

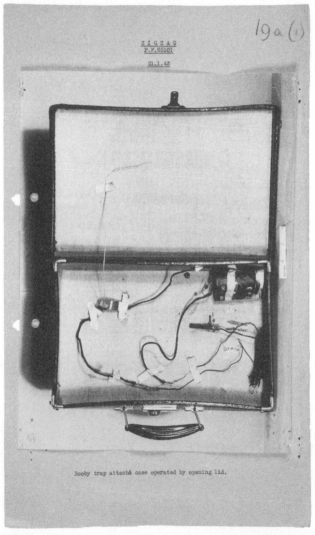

Photo of the bomb in Agent Zigzag's attaché case supplied by the Germans.

SPYDLE CHALLENGE

Imagine you are trying to track down four briefcases which you believe have been rigged with explosive devices. They are each a different colour on the outside, each is being carried by an agent of a different nationality and each is being transported to a different city. Use the following clues, along with the chart, to complete the table at the bottom of the page:

- The Finnish agent does not have a blue briefcase
- Barcelona is where the German is heading
- Limoges is the destination of the French carrier
- The black briefcase is with either the German or the Portuguese carrier
- The blue briefcase is not heading to Antwerp, and not being carried by the German
- The French carrier has a brown briefcase

	Agent's Nationality				Destination			
	Finnish	French	German	Portuguese	Antwerp	Barcelona	Copenhagen	Limoges
Black								
Blue								
Brown								
Red								
Antwerp								
Barcelona								
Copenhagen								
Limoges								

Briefcase Colour	Agent's Nationality	Destination

129: CANNED BADS

Explosives could be hidden in all manner of everyday items, such as this item of German sabotage equipment, which was disguised as canned 'food'. It was intercepted in Turkey en route for Syria in August 1943.

Photograph of a food tin used to disguise incendiary devices provided to German agents during the Second World War.

SPYDLE CHALLENGE

The image opposite shows a tin of plums used to disguise German sabotage materials. Use your linguistic and deductive skills to reveal the one-word name of a French culinary dish, cans of which were also used to disguise explosive devices. Jumbled up in the circle below are the letters of the dish, which can be formed by using each letter exactly once.

How many additional words can you then form that use the centre letter plus two or more of the other letters? No letter may be used more times than it appears within the circle. There are over 120 additional words to find, not including proper nouns.

130: HIDDEN WIRES

The image below shows how it was not just explosives that were disguised in everyday items. Here, a wireless transmission device has been camouflaged by hiding it in an innocuous bundle of sticks.

Photograph of a wireless set camouflaged in a bundle of sticks, 1944.

SPYDLE CHALLENGE

Use your tracking skills to reveal six items, each listed in the same Second-World-War document that contained the picture of the cyclist opposite, which could be used to camouflage or hide wireless devices. Starting at the top-left square below, find a path that visits every grid square. As it travels, the path must spell out the name of each item. The path can only travel horizontally or vertically between squares, and must finish on the bottom row. The first three items, as well as the final item, each consist of two words.

P	A	I	N	O	X	B	A
B	R	A	T	B	R	H	T
A	T	C	S	E	O	O	M
E	T	F	T	L	A	C	S
R	R	I	W	O	O	D	G
Y	D	H	P	O	M	A	R
E	N	O	U	M	E	A	N
V	A	C	U	C	L	R	E

131: THE WIRELESS DEPARTMENT

The Special Operations Executive (SOE) recorded some of their intelligence work, including this photograph album with images of an exhibition of the work of SOE Station 15b. The exhibition was put on display in the 'Demonstration Room' gallery of the Natural History Museum. Exhibits included some of the equipment developed by Station 15b to be used to carry out covert operations behind enemy lines.

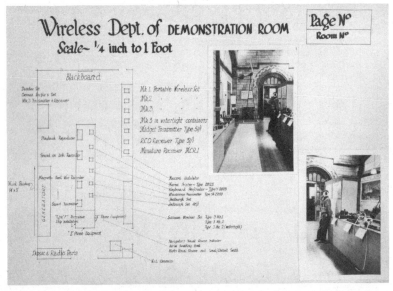

Photograph of the Wireless Department of Station 15b, as shown in an exhibition.

SPYDLE CHALLENGE

Use your code-cracking skills to reveal the names of nine European cities which have each been transmitted in Morse code. You also know that:

- .... .   -- .- - .- ... .-. .- .-..

.... - --- .-. ----   -- ..- ... . .-- --

. . . is a Morse representation of 'THE NATURAL HISTORY MUSEUM'. Given this, which nine cities are indicated by the Morse code below? There is one per line.

- --- .-- .-. --- .- ... .

.-. --- -- .

.- .- .-. .... .- ...

-- .. .-. .- -.

.-.. .. .-. .-. .

.- - .... . -. ...

.- .-. -- . .-. .. .-

--- ... .-. ---

-- .- .-. ... .-. .-. .

132: TIME TO NAME NAMES

The map below is taken from a document dated 1944–45, which gives the details and geographical locations of several agents working in the Netherlands.

SOE war diary operational map showing the Netherlands, with names of zones, regions and commanders.

SPYDLE CHALLENGE

Many agents listed in the document above are identified using their official codenames along with two additional codenames – a 'training' name, and a 'field' name – along with a particular location in the Netherlands. Use your deductive skills and the chart and clues below to work out the training and field names given to each of the four agents listed in the table, along with the Dutch location each is associated with. These are all taken directly from the document.

- TAZELAAR is not in Veluwe
- WHIMPER is not the same person as VICTOR
- SCHEFFER is either in Rotterdam or also known as JIM – but not both
- VICTOR and SCHEFFER are the same person
- NECKING is not known as PALSTRA
- Amsterdam is not the location of BENDER
- Rotterdam is not where SPLASH can be found
- JIM is not BENDER
- NECKING is either also known as TAZELAAR, or in Amsterdam – but not both
- SPLASH is not also known as FRED
- JIM is not known as NECKING
- TONY is not the agent also known as BENDER

Codename	Training Name	Field Name	Location

133: CONVINCING FAKES

The forgery of documents during the Second World War saved many lives. In Nazi-occupied territories, skilled forgers operated clandestinely, in places ranging from resistance hideouts to prisoner of war camps. Many members of the resistance were taught the skills necessary to be able to fake identity cards, passports, ration cards, work permits and other documents. In Britain the military intelligence division responsible for evasion and escape (MI9) produced samples of forgeries in their training manuals.

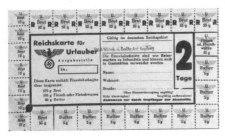

Examples of forged documents taken from an SOE war diary used by agents in the field: a German ration card and Dutch identity cards.

SPYDLE CHALLENGE

Imagine you are in charge of issuing forged documents to agents in the field. There are three types of document for you to distribute, each for a different purpose: essential, corroborative or emergency. You need to distribute the right document to the correct codenamed agent, each of which is in a different location. Use the clues and chart below, along with your deductive skills, to work out which agents need which documents, for which purpose – and where to send them.

- CRUX is either in need of a corroborative document or at The Hague – but not both
- FLANNEL needs the identity card, but is not in Rotterdam
- The corroborative document is the theatre ticket
- The identity card either is needed at The Hague or is the emergency document – but not both
- Rotterdam is not where the theatre ticket is required

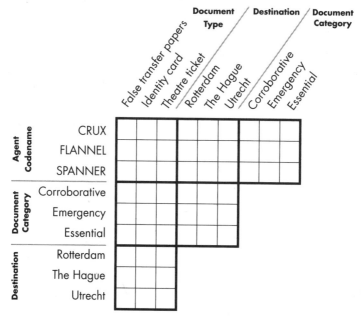

Agent Codename	Document Type	Document Category	Destination

134: MULTIPLE IDENTITIES

This document reveals the different names given to undercover agents Gurgle and Rumble, who were part of the Dutch SOE. Their second mission took place only weeks before the end of the Second World War in Europe was declared.

GURGLE & RUMBLE (Second Mission)   (Liaison in Noord Holland)

      GURGLE's training name was BROEKMAN. He would be known in the field as DIRK.

      RUMBLE's training name was PLEYSIER. He would be known in the field as KLAAS.

      London had no direct liaison with the N.B.S. in Noord Holland, north of the Noord Zee canal.

      According to information received from the Commander, the N.B.S. was about 1,450 strong in that area. Weapons and explosives had already been dropped in Noord Holland.

GURGLE

GURGLE and RUMBLE would act as liaison officers between the Commander of the N.B.S. in Noord Holland and the Allied forces.

      They would assist in the organisation of reception of arms and explosives and give instructions in their use.

      They would assist the Commander of the N.B.S. in Noord Holland in the organising of his forces for the execution in due course of the orders which had already been transmitted to him.

      GRIND, SPLASH, YELP, GURGLE and RUMBLE (Second Mission) were dropped on the night of April 23rd, but owing to the food dropping and the German capitulation their mission was short-lived.

SOE war diary entry on Dutch agents Gurgle and Rumble.

SPYDLE CHALLENGE

Each of the codenames below has been taken from the war diary shown opposite, which details the codenames and activities of agents in the Netherlands during the Second World War. Fit all of these codenames once each into the grid below, one letter per square, so they each read either across or down.

3-letter words	5-letter words	6-letter words	7-letter words	9-letter words
AAT	FLUIT	DEKKER	BERNARD	BOBSLEIGH
BOS	GRUNT	FOKKER	SNOOKER	CORNELIUS
DON	KLAAS	GURGLE		SJOERDSMA
EDU	LOUIS	JINGLE	8-letter words	
	PODEX	RUMBLE	BROEKMAN	
4-letter words	RUMMY	SCREAM	COURSING	
DIRK	SNORT	SQUEAK	PLEYSIER	
HISS		STUVEL	TRAPPING	
JOOP				
ROLF				

— SOLUTIONS —

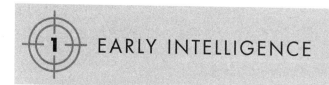

EARLY INTELLIGENCE

1: THE BAG OF SECRETS

The letters can be rearranged to spell ANNE BOLEYN, the second wife of King Henry VIII, whose trial documents were kept in the *Baga de Secretis*.
Words that can be found in the circle of letters include able, ale, aloe, alone, anyone, aye, bale, baleen, baloney, bane, bean, bee, been, belay, bole, bone, bye, ebony, eel, enable, ennoble, eon, eye, lane, lea, lean, lee, lobe, lone, lye, nee, neon, noble, noel, none, obey, one, yea and yen.

2: HIDDEN HEARINGS

City Reported From	Report Overheard	Hiding Place
Seville	New king is weak	Lavatory
Avignon	Queen is unfaithful	Pantry
Porto	A coup is likely	Wardrobe

3: TUDOR TROUBLE

The message has been disguised by writing each individual word backwards. The King of Spain warned that 'Secrecy is necessary in great enterprises and that nothing should be written except in cipher'.

4: VENETIAN SECRETS

The names have been encoded by shifting each vowel one place 'forward' in the set of five vowels. A has become E, E has become I, and so on, until U has become A. The names of the ten city-states are therefore:

SALERNO	PISA
GAETA	AMALFI
GENOA	RAGUSA
ANCONA	NOLI
SIENA	CALABRIA

VENICE, encoded in the same way, would become 'VINOCI'.

5: A CUNNING DISGUISE

Place Sent To	Language Spoken	Merchant Wares
Marseille	French	Cloth
Annecy	Flemish	Spices
Rouen	Dutch	Jewellery

6: EXPENSIVE ASSETS

Sir Gilbert Talbot's first payment was for £104 – equivalent to over £110,000 in 2024.

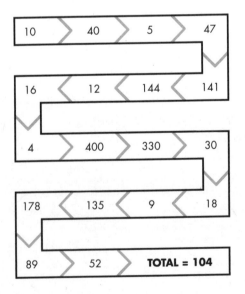

7: SPINELLY'S SPY

The port reports should be ordered as follows:

1. Cadiz
2. Faro
3. Cascais
4. Peniche
5. Oporto
6. Bilbao
7. Bayonne
8. Brest

8: SPIES AND SUSPICIONS

The clues can be solved as follows:

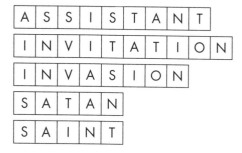

The name given to a spying excursion was therefore a VISITATION.

9: FABRICATED FELONIES

Institution	Relic	Debt
Kaldham Monalium	Finger of St Stephen	20 marks
Selby	Belt of St Mary	300 pounds
Grace Dien Monalium	Tunic of St Thomas	20 pounds

10: SPY SCHOOL

Recruited from	Trained in	Dispatched to
Oxford University	Forgery	Spain
Cambridge University	Decryption	France
London	Languages	Belgium

11: ENEMIES OF THE CROWN

The quote has been disguised with an 'Atbash' cipher, which means that the letters of the alphabet have been replaced with their opposite positional counterparts – so A is replaced with Z, and B is replaced with Y, and so on through until Y is replaced with B and Z with A. The complete quote from Thomas Morgan is therefore as follows:

'THERE BE MANY MEANS IN HAND TO REMOVE THE BEAST THAT TROUBLES THE WORLD'

12: SEALED BY A SPY

Destination	Code	Month
France	Zodiac	May
Scotland	Number	June
Spain	Alphabetical	October

13: DOUBLE AGENT

The message has been disguised by replacing each letter of the alphabet with a number representing its position. Sometimes in a code of this type A=1, B=2, C=3 and so on. In this particular code, however, all of the numbers have then been doubled – which explains why they are all even. The message therefore reads:

'I have **HEARD** of the **WORK** you do and I want to **SERVE** you. I have no **SCRUPLES** and no **FEAR** of **DANGER**. Whatever you **ORDER** me to do I will **ACCOMPLISH**.'

14: MARY'S CIPHERS

Symbol	Position	Country
♁	Queen	England
♡	Prince	Scotland
‡	King	Spain

the k. of Spane

the Pr: of Scotland

the Q. of England.

15: THE NAMES OF TRAITORS

The names and their associated 'intercepting' treasonous words are as follows:

BALLARD + TRAITOR
TICHBORNE + TURNCOAT
SALISBURY + BETRAYER
DONN + SPY
BARNEWELL + CONSPIRATOR
SAVAGE + PLOTTER

16: A FLEXIBLE TRAITOR

Destination	Transport	Objective
Brussels	Boat	Collect gold
Rome	Horseback	Visit colleagues
Madrid	On foot	Seek out new business
London	Carriage	Purchase new property

17: BEWARE EAVESDROPPERS

The path can be traced as follows:

This reveals that the person to whom Ridolfi told his plot was: Cosimo I de Medici, Grand Duke of Tuscany.

18: SPIES IN SPAIN

Asset	Number
Galleons	25
Spanish soldiers	16,000
Italian soldiers	12,000
German soldiers	10,000
Horses	1,000

19: ALSO KNOWN AS

The clues can be solved as follows:

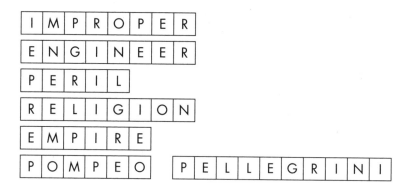

Antony Standen's pseudonym was therefore POMPEO PELLEGRINI. The full code is shown below:

1	2	3	4	5	6	7	8	9
P	O	M	E	L	G	R	I	N

Signature of Standen as Pompeo Pellegrini.

20: MAKING TRACKS

The stopovers will be made in the following order:

1. Thetford
2. Hengrave
3. Shelford
4. Royston
5. Hatfield
6. Harrow
7. Hampton Court

All of these places are named on the document shown opposite the puzzle page.

2 TREASON, PLOT AND REVOLUTION

21: JUICY GOSSIP

The missing letters can be filled in to reveal the following words, which are all citrus fruits:

L E M(O)N

T A N G E(R)I N E

S A T S U M(A)

C L E M E(N)T I N E

(G)R A P E F R U I T

L I M(E)

The circled letters spell ORANGE, the fruit whose juice was used as invisible ink. It fades on drying, and only becomes visible once the paper is warmed. Garnett used this technique to communicate with his friends and associates while he was imprisoned in the Tower of London; as the orange juice remained visible after it had been warmed it would indicate whether the letter had been intercepted and read or not.

22: SURROUNDED BY LIES

The word using all of the letters is SPECTACLES.

The decoy message was wrapped around a pair of glasses, and the opening message reads *'lett these spectacles be set in leather...'*.

The five clued words are:

1. Castle
2. Escape
3. Elect
4. Pact
5. Peace

Other words to find include: accept, accepts, access, ace, aces, act, acts, aspect, aspects, cap, cape, capes, caplet, caplets, caps, case, cases, cast, caste, castes, castles, casts, cat, cats, cease, ceases, celesta, celestas, clap, claps, clasp, clasps, class, cleat, cleats, elects, escapes, lace, laces, pace, paces, pacts, peaces, place, places, sac, sacs, scale, scales, scalp, scalps, sect, sects, select, selects, space, spaces, spec, specs, spectacle and talc.

23: A WORD OF WARNING

The recipient of the letter was Lord MONTEAGLE:

M	E	G	N	A	O	L	R	T
R	O	A	G	T	L	N	E	M
L	T	N	E	R	M	A	G	O
N	M	O	T	L	R	E	A	G
T	A	L	M	E	G	R	O	N
E	G	R	O	N	A	T	M	L
O	R	E	L	M	N	G	T	A
G	N	T	A	O	E	M	L	R
A	L	M	R	G	T	O	N	E

24: HIDDEN HERETICS

'Percy' is hiding in the following location:

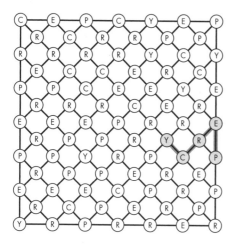

25: CONFESSION TIME

1. Wintour
2. Wright the Elder
3. Wright the Younger
4. Rokewood
5. Catesby and Percy

26: THE WAR ON TRUTH

R	S	E	D	H	N	A	U	O
H	O	D	A	U	S	N	E	R
N	A	U	E	O	R	D	S	H
O	R	H	N	E	U	S	D	A
U	E	A	S	D	O	H	R	N
S	D	N	R	A	H	U	O	E
D	N	O	U	R	A	E	H	S
E	H	S	O	N	D	R	A	U
A	U	R	H	S	E	O	N	D

The cause supported by the *Mercurius Civicus* paper was the ROUNDHEAD cause – that is, the parliamentary one.

27: REBEL REPORTS

Order of Report	Name	Place
1	Sir Thomas Middleton	Chester
2	Sir Thomas Fairfax	Yorkshire
3	Earle of Manchester	Lincolnshire
4	Prince de Harcourt	House of Commons

You can find these names and locations in a page from *The Kingdomes Weekly Post*:

(119)

the City and Parliament to obferve the motions of their Prince, and to looke well about in the feafon of fuch approaches.

Newcaftle hath difpatched in Derbyfhire, and is returned into Yorkfhire, his grand bufineffe was like that of Prince *Ruperts, firing* and *Plundering*, his Army is not very confiderable, you may fee what a mighty Marqueffe may come to in time.

Hopton they fay fends out his *Warrants* in his own name for the Countrey to come in, and in fuch a high ftile as if he had forgotten who is King this yeare.

Sir *William* Brereton, and Sir *Thomas Middleton*, and their Army are all rifen from *Chefter*, thefe may informe them with fome *Field-piaces* and Colverings a little better in the Proteftant Religion.

Sir *Thomas Fairfax* they fay is marched up to Sir *William* Breretons affiftance, it is not much out of the way into Yorkfhire if he fucceed.

The Earle of *Manchefters* forces, with Colonell *Cromwells*, are about *Sleaforth* in Lincolnfhire, I hope they are confidering of another Victory, and how to give *Hinderfon* a fecond part of a routing.

Poole in Dorfetfhire hath done excellent fervice of late in feverall defeats upon the enemy, which fummed up, will make a confiderable Conqueft.

The *Counfell at Oxford* hath now almoft loft *Ireland*, his Majefty is plainly cheated of one *Scepter*, and the Rebels have taken it into their owne hands, but it feemes the Pope tooke it ill to fee a Prince as *triple Diadem'd* as himfelfe, and thinkes fuch Kings are too neare his owne *Supremacy*, and therefore he would eafe him of one Crowne.

Prince *De Harcourt* defires more entercourfe with the Parliament, but he goes about to the houfe of Commons, and

28: A SONG OF SEDITION

The first and last letters of each word have been swapped. The complete line of the song therefore reads: 'NO MORE SHALL FOREIGN SCUM POLLUTE OUR THRONE'.

29: PORTSMOUTH PLANS

Name	Profession	Location
William Dunster	Tailor	Deptford
Thomas Figgins	Shoemaker	Portsmouth
Mr Woodcock	Unknown profession	Fleet Street
Henry Page	Excise Office	Unknown location

30: DOUBLE TROUBLE

The words can be placed as follows:

The name of the possible double agent is therefore JOHN ERSKINE, the Earl of Mar.

31: A SORRY CIPHER

The ciphered text reads 'ALL THE PEOPLE BELIEVE SHE WAS POISONED'.

Each letter has been replaced by a number indicating that letter's position in the alphabet, but with the alphabet reversed so it runs from Z to A. Therefore, A has been replaced with 26, and B with 25, and so on until Z (if it had appeared) would have been replaced with 1. This is not the exact code used in the original letter, although it did involve numbers.

32: COFFEE CULTURE

Coffee House Codename	Area of London	Foreign Spy Nationality
King	Soho	Canadian
Banner	Westminster	French
Anthem	Greenwich	Moroccan
Duty	Covent Garden	Turkish

33: BATTLE BREAKERS

Battle Location	Year	Defeated Leader
Oporto	1809	Soult
Salamanca	1812	Marmont
Vittoria	1813	Joseph Bonaparte

34: THE SPY SCOVELL

The anagrams can be solved as follows:

SPANISH + G
PORTUGUESE + U
IRISH + I
SWISS + D
ITALIAN + E

The extra letters spell GUIDE, for these soldiers were known as Army Guides.

35: EXPLORING OFFICERS

Officer Codename	Skill	Task
Red	Horseman	Count enemy troops
White	Draughtsman	Record enemy movements
Blue	Linguist	Intercept letters

36: SCOVELL'S SCOPE

The Great Cipher was based on 1,400 numbers:

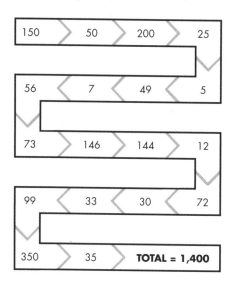

37: THE BROKEN CODE

The clues can be solved as follows:

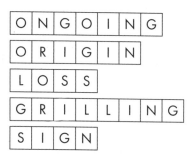

R	O	S	S	I	G	N	O	L

The family was the ROSSIGNOL family. The full code is shown below:

1	2	3	4	5	6	7
R	O	S	I	G	N	L

38: CRYPTOGRAPHY CLASSES

Language	Code type	Point of Weakness
Latin	Substitution	Vowels
Dutch	Index	Short words
German	Transposition	Letter sign-offs

39: INDEXICAL INTELLIGENCE

The book needed to crack Scovell's code was a DICTIONARY. Other words to find include: any, arid, diction, din, don, dory, dot, idiot, ion, iron, irony, nary, nit, nod, nor, not, ran, ray, rid, riot, rod, rot, tin, tiny, ton, tony, tor, torn and yarn.

40: GRIDS AND GRAPHEMES

The clues can be solved as follows:

GAUGE
ILLEGAL
AREA
LIAR
IRREGULAR

The final word is therefore GUERRILLA.

GUERRILLA warfare was used by the Spanish and Portuguese populations who opposed Napoleon's expansion into Iberia.

The full code is:

⅂	<	☐	⌐•	⌐	⌊•	⌋
G	U	E	R	I	L '	A

41: AN OFFICER AND A GENTLEMAN

1. Valencia
2. Talavera
3. Madrid
4. Cadiz
5. Albuera
6. Corunna
7. Lisbon
8. Bailen

42: RANK FOR RANK

The correct transcript is as follows, with the un-swapped words marked in bold:

> I, the undersigned, Colquhoun Grant, **Major** in the 11th Regiment of the English infantry, taken prisoner of war by the **French** army on the 16th of **April** 1812, undertake on my **parole** of honour not to **seek** to escape or to remove myself from the place of my **captivity** without permission, and not to **pass** any intelligence to the **English** army and its allies; in fact, not to depart in any way from the duties which an officer **prisoner** of war on parole is honour bound to **perform**; and not to serve against the French army and its allies until I have been **exchanged**, rank for rank.
>
> **Portugal** 17 April 1812.

Nevertheless, Grant escaped his parole and passed himself off as an American officer, travelling to Paris with a French general. In Paris, still in the guise of an American and now even closer to Napoleon, he sent many messages to Wellington in Spain. He returned to England and eventually rejoined Wellington at the front, continuing to serve as a senior intelligence officer for many years.

43: KIEL CANAL

The words can be fit into the grid as follows:

The letters in the shaded squares can be rearranged to spell SUBMARINE.

44: A NEW DIVISION

The word which uses all the letters, and forms the name of the government department, is Admiralty. Other words to find include: admiral, admit, aid, ail, aim, air, airy, alarm, altar, amid, amity, aria, arid, arm, army, art, arty, atria, daily, dairy, dam, dart, data, day, dial, diary, dram, drama, dray, lad, lady, laid, lair, laity, lam, lama, lard, lariat, lay, liar, lira, mad, madly, maid, mail, malady, malt, mar, marital, mart, martial, mat, may, myriad, radial, raid, rail, ram, rat, ray, tail, tam, tar, tardily, tardy, tiara, tidal, trail, tram, tray, triad, trial, yam and yard.

45: DETERMINED DEFENCE

Coast Section	Defences	Nearby Terrain
North	Fortified pier	Rocky
East	Barracks	Sandy
South	Battery	Tree-covered
West	Submarine nets	Grassland

46: HIDING IN PLAIN SIGHT

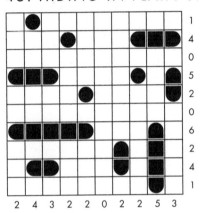

47: LUCKY ACQUISITIONS

M	E	R	U	B	S	A	G	D
U	A	D	M	G	R	E	B	S
S	B	G	E	A	D	R	U	M
G	R	B	D	U	M	S	E	A
A	D	S	R	E	G	B	M	U
E	M	U	A	S	B	G	D	R
D	S	M	G	R	E	U	A	B
B	G	A	S	D	U	M	R	E
R	U	E	B	M	A	D	S	G

The name of the ship was the MAGDEBURG.

48: SHARING IS CARING

Name of Book	Coastal Area Found	Found by Whom
Signalbuch der Kaiserlichen Marine (SKM)	Estonia	Russian forces
Handelsverkehrsbuch (HVB)	Australia	Royal Navy
Verkehrsbuch (VB)	Netherlands	British trawler

49: AREAS OF INTEREST

The sea areas will be targeted in the following order:

1. Dogger
2. Wight
3. Forth
4. Tyne
5. Forties
6. Fisher
7. Humber
8. Thames

50: NO SIGNS OF REMORSE

The names of the towns are:

BOURNEMOUTH
FALMOUTH
PORTSMOUTH
SOUTHPORT
TYNEMOUTH
WEYMOUTH

51: TRAFFIC ANALYSIS

Signal Source	Likely Target	Order of Attack
Scorpion	Willow	1
Arrow	Star	2
Hammer	Cormorant	3
Snake	Breeze	4

52: FOILED BY FOLIAGE

The items and trees can be revealed as follows:

CAMP + ASH
TRENCH + WILLOW
PIER + BEECH
HOWITZER + CHESTNUT
STREAM + CYPRESS
ROAD + OAK

53: COUNTING CAMPSITES

Grid Square Reference	No. of Tents	No. of Guns
224	20	8
202	15	28
203	732	14
196	0	25

54: DIRE STRAITS

B	H	R	T	U	D	O	S	P
T	O	D	H	S	P	U	B	R
U	P	S	O	R	B	D	H	T
R	U	H	P	D	T	S	O	B
D	B	O	S	H	R	T	P	U
S	T	P	U	B	O	H	R	D
P	S	T	B	O	U	R	D	H
H	R	B	D	T	S	P	U	O
O	D	U	R	P	H	B	T	S

The name of the strait is the BOSPHORUS.

55: SUBTLE SUBTERFUGE

The readings reveal that there are 20 submarines in this sea area:

🛥	2	🛥	2	1		🛥	1
2	4	2		🛥	3	1	
🛥	2	🛥	4	🛥	2		1
2	3	3	🛥	3		1	🛥
🛥			🛥		1		2
3	4	🛥	3	🛥			🛥
🛥	🛥	3		2	3	2	
🛥	4	🛥	2	🛥	2	🛥	1

56: TERRITORIAL TEMPTATIONS

The three missing US states are NEW MEXICO, ARIZONA and TEXAS. The rest of the states can be found as shown below:

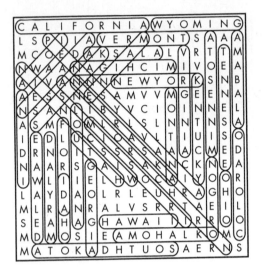

57: FOR YOUR EYES ONLY

Order of Preference	Explanation	Means of Notifying
1	Document leaked in Mexico	Telephone call
2	Document leaked in Germany	Telegram
3	Document intercepted in US	Letter

58: THE SOUND OF A SPY

Each letter of the alphabet from A to J has been assigned a position on the musical 'stave', with 'A' occupying the lowest position, as can be seen from the example. The notes therefore translate to letters as follows:

A B C D E F G H I

The codenames can in turn be decoded as follows:

ACADIA
GIGI
EDDIE
HEIDI
CHIEF – who is presumably the most important

59: MUSICAL MASK

Composer	Destination	Contents
Mozart	Berlin	General strike launched
Bach	Dresden	Location of a factory
Beethoven	Hamburg	Troop movements
Strauss	Munich	Financial accounts

60: A CALL TO ARMS

The topic mentioned is CONSCRIPTION.
Other words to find include: con, cons, conscript, coo, coop, coos, coot, cop, cot, icon, icons, ins, into, ion, ions, nip, noon, not, onto, opt, optic, pin, pins, pint, pot, print, rip, scrip, script, snip, snoop, snoot, son, soon, soot, sop, sot, ton, tons, too and top.

61: BIT BY BIT

The Morse-like symbols on the right show you which letters to use from each of the words on the left, with dashes indicating a letter to be ignored and dots indicating a letter to be selected. Each group of 'Morse' dots and dashes corresponds with a word on the left, based on their corresponding positions on the page. The selected letters can be appended in usual reading order to reveal MEETMEATNINE. Adding spaces in (based on the most likely reading) then reveals the sentence 'Meet me at nine'.

62: THE BITTER END

The complete words are:

SOLDIER
CADET
OFFICER
REGULAR
SENTRY
MARINE
RIFLEMAN

63: A DELICATE DANCE

The clues can be solved as follows:

S	C	A	N	D	A	L		

D	A	M	S	E	L	

S	E	E	M	L	I	N	E	S	S

A	S	S	A	S	S	I	N

A	C	C	L	A	I	M	E	D

The world-famous venue is therefore, in French, LA SCALA DE MILAN – the internationally renowned opera house, La Scala.

64: A SEQUENCE OF SPIES

The contacts from each of the cities were met in the following order:

1. Brussels
2. Madrid
3. Milan
4. Paris
5. Dublin
6. Smyrna
7. Rome
8. Geneva

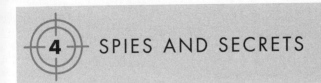

65: TREASURED ASSET

Real name	Codename	Nationality
Eddie Hultz	PRINCE	Italian
Gertrude Stola	HERON	French
Jon Merson	CRUX	Russian
Martha Johannes	BLOSSOM	German

66: CARBON COPIES

The names can be deciphered as follows:

CHAOS
ATLAS
URANUS
HYPERION
ARTEMIS
HERA

All of the names are derived from Greek mythology.

67: RIGHT-HAND WOMAN

The secret message is shown below, with the cover message faded out:

The cover message reads 'LOVELY WEATHER IN BRIGHTON WISH YOU WERE HERE SPEAK SOON'. The secret message is 'MORE TROOPS ON THE WAY STAND BY FOR NUMBERS SHORTLY'.

68: A SPY'S SIGN-OFF

The clues can be solved as follows:

S	O	L	O	
A	L	O	N	E
A	S	S	E	S	S
G	L	E	A	N
S	A	G	E	

Treasure's official sign-off was therefore SOLANGE, to be used with her German handlers.

69: LAYING THE TRAIL

Location	Codename	Troops	Mobilization
South coast	WINNER	10,000	By land
East coast	PLATINUM	14,000	By sea
North coast	TROPHY	12,000	By air

70: HIGH PRAISE

The name of the department is the GOVERNMENT CODE AND CYPHER SCHOOL, which can be found as follows:

The department is now known as GCHQ (**G**overnment **C**ommunications **H**ead**q**uarters).

71: A LITTLE OFF-TRACK

Treasure's dog, Babs, had been left in GIBRALTAR:

G	A	T	B	R	D	I	S	L
L	I	D	A	S	T	B	R	G
R	S	B	L	I	G	D	T	A
I	D	G	R	B	S	A	L	T
T	R	L	G	A	I	S	D	B
S	B	A	D	T	L	R	G	I
A	G	I	S	L	R	T	B	D
D	T	R	I	G	B	L	A	S
B	L	S	T	D	A	G	I	R

72: THE PRICE OF LOYALTY

Treasure was offered £5 a week – roughly equivalent to £185 in 2024:

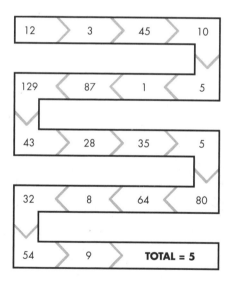

12	3	45	10
129	87	1	5
43	28	35	5
32	8	64	80
54	9	**TOTAL = 5**	

73: CROSSING THE LINE

The clues can be solved as follows:

O	M	I	T		

Q	U	I	T		

M	O	T	T	O	

O	U	S	T		

S	U	M	M	I	T

The name of the aircraft is therefore the MOSQUITO.

74: A TALE OF DECEIT

You are describing the activities as taking place in the following order:

1. Comms interception
2. Language class
3. Fitness training
4. Meeting with handler
5. Reconnaissance
6. Filing case report
7. Dead letter drop
8. Falsifying documents

75: SELF-SABOTAGE

Location in Building	Damage	Cause
North wing	Collapsed ceiling	Burst water main
Main warehouse	Hole in outer wall	Arson
Loading bay	Smoke damage	Electricity cables cut

76: LOOSE CANNON

Recipient's Codename	Information Leaked	Recipient's Nationality
Marrow	Double agent's codename	Dutch
Blunt	Plans for next mission	Norwegian
Cooper	Report of previous mission	German
Tricky	Name of agent's handler	French

77: HE SAID, HE SAID

Russet is the traitor. Both Russet and Milton accuse Frank of being the occasional liar – but for this to be true, one of them would have to be the steadfast liar who was being truthful, which is a logical impossibility. They are therefore both lying, meaning that Frank must be the one who always tells the truth. Frank's statement can then be taken as true – that Milton occasionally lies but occasionally doesn't – leaving Russet as the one who always lies.

78: RESPONSIBLE OFFICER

Agent Codename	Mission Codename	Task to Complete
MARIGOLD	OVERTHROW	Provide passport
VERONICA	DISCOMBOBULATE	Issue false visas
AZALEA	UNDERMINE	Procure enemy uniform
MAGNOLIA	FLUMMOX	Arrange flight

79: KEEPING MUM

The name of the technique is PROVOCATION. Other words to find include: acorn, act, action, actor, air, ant, anti, antic, apricot, apron, apt, arc, art, atop, cairn, can, cant, canto, cantor, cap, caption, captor, car, carp, cart, carton, cartoon, cat, cation, catnip, cavort, coat, copra, corona, inapt, iota, nap, nova, oar, oration, ova, ovation, pact, pain, paint, pair, pan, panic, pant, par, part, pat, patio, patron, piano, pica, pita, rain, ran, rant, rap, rapt, rat, ratio, ration, roan, taco, tan, tap, tapir, tar, taro, tarpon, train, trap, vain, van, vat, via, vicar and vocation.

80: SPILLING THE BEANS

Real Forename	Codename	Age	Destination
Charles	Banjo	21	Antwerp
Mark	Cricket	19	Paris
Peter	Penguin	24	Calais
John	Marble	22	Brest

81: MAKING CONTACT

The words can be filled in as follows:

S	T	R	E	S	S

S	E	E	K

T	R	U	E

M	U	T	T	E	R

M	E	E	K

The name of the underground group is therefore the MUSKETEERS.

82: THE MOTIVE

The words can be fit into the grid as follows:

The letters in the shaded squares can be rearranged to reveal that Khan's motive appeared to have been IDEALISM. You can see the original copy of the report below:

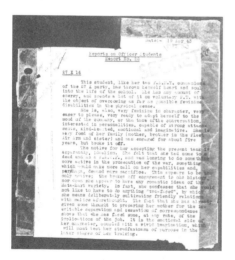

83: WIRELESS MISSIONS

Codename	'Pass' Word	City
MORTON	Hijinks	Birmingham
WHITTLE	Clamour	Manchester
FARRIER	Tenacity	Liverpool
HEMLOCK	Windbreak	London

84: A WOMAN OF MANY NAMES

The names have been encoded with a shift of +5. To decode them, each letter must be shifted 5 places earlier in the alphabet. The names are therefore as follows:

Codename in the field: MARIE
Nickname she gave to her prosthetic leg: CUTHBERT
Nickname given to her by the Germans: THE LIMPING LADY
Additional nickname given to her by the Germans: ARTEMIS
Nickname given to her by fellow SOE agents: MARIE OF LYON
Codename used by downed airmen when seeking her help: OLIVIER

85: WHAT'S IN A NAME?

Real Name	Field Name	Cover Surname
Noor Inayat Khan	Madeleine	Renier
Eliane Plewman	Gaby	Prunier
Virginia Hall	Diane	Montagne

The full cover names of each agent were:

Noor Inayat Khan: Jeanne Marie Renier
Eliane Plewman: Eliane Jacqueline Prunier
Virginia Hall: Marcelle Montagne

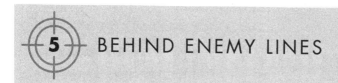

86: OVERHEAD OPERATIONS

From above, the structures would appear as follows:

The name of the operation was 'CROSSBOW'.

87: UNDER THE RADAR

The geographical features and vehicles can be separated as follows:

TANK + COVE
DREADNOUGHT + ARCHIPELAGO
SUBMARINE + MOUNTAIN
WARSHIP + VOLCANO
AEROPLANE + CANYON
GUNBOAT + FJORD
HELICOPTER + GLACIER
DESTROYER + ISTHMUS
MINESWEEPER + ISLAND
SEAPLANE + LAGOON

Location Codename	Number of Troops	Assets Sighted
LYNX	1,000	Tanks
THORN	2,400	Aircraft
DUNE	1,200	Anti-tank guns
PANTHER	1,800	Gun battery

89: SPECIAL SERVICES

The name can be found as follows:

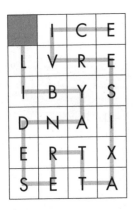

The nickname given to the LRDG was therefore the 'Libyan Desert Taxi Service'.

90: TERMS OF ENGAGEMENT

The clues can be solved as follows:

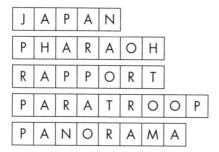

J	A	P	A	N				
P	H	A	R	A	O	H		
R	A	P	P	O	R	T		
P	A	R	A	T	R	O	O	P
P	A	N	O	R	A	M	A	

Stirling's nickname was therefore the 'Phantom Major'.

91: HARD LANDING

The items can be revealed as follows:

P	A	R	R	N	E	S	S
N	I	A	A	H	E	R	C
G	Y	C	H	U	T	A	S
S	L	F	T	E	M	L	H
U	P	I	S	T	O	E	H
I	T	A	R	T	L	F	O
E	T	N	S	L	R	A	O
R	T	I	M	E	C	P	D

The items described in the article are therefore:

PARACHUTE

HARNESS

CRASH HELMET

FLYING SUIT

PISTOL

FOOD PARCEL

TRANSMITTER

92: SUFFICIENT SUPPLIES

The items can be placed as follows:

The highlighted letters can be rearranged to spell ST ALBANS.

93: LOCATED IN PART

The places can be unscrambled as follows:

Location Richter claimed to have just arrived from:
IPSWICH

Other locations Richter claimed to have visited:
CROMER
NORWICH
CAMBRIDGE
BURY ST EDMUNDS

Country of Richter's birth, according to his passport:
CZECHOSLOVAKIA

94: SKETCHY SURVEILLANCE

Item	Location Buried	Order of Discovery
Codebook	Pond	1
Transmitter	Wood	2
Fake passport	Haystack	3
Map of targets	Well	4

95: KEEPING AN EYE OUT

The clues can be solved as follows:

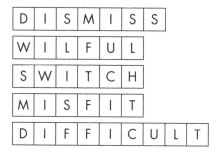

D	I	S	M	I	S	S	

W	I	L	F	U	L	

S	W	I	T	C	H	

M	I	S	F	I	T	

D	I	F	F	I	C	U	L	T

The name of the agent that Richter was sent to check up on was therefore WULF SCHMIDT.

96: A VERY TALL TALE

The events happened in the following order – supposedly:

1. Parachuted into Budapest
2. Arrested in Gdansk
3. Airlifted to Vienna
4. Injured in Lisbon
5. Imprisoned in Utrecht
6. Trained in Paris
7. Escaped to Prague
8. Recruited in Madrid
9. Deported from Rome

97: APPEARANCE IS EVERYTHING

The jumbled words are:

Build: THIN
Hair: DARK BLONDE
Nose: FAT and PENDULOUS
Face: SMALL and THIN
Dressed: SHABBILY
Gait: Walks with DROOPING shoulders
Languages: GERMAN, FRENCH and ARABIC

98: EXPEDITIOUS ENCOUNTERS

The locations were encountered in the following order, as can be seen on the map below:

1. GIALO
2. SAND DUNES
3. SIGHEN
4. KEBABO
5. GILF EL KEBIR
6. DAKBLA KARGA
7. ASYUT

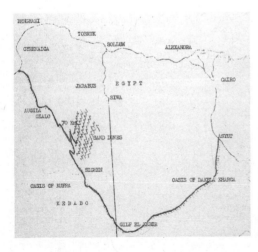

The original map showing routes and sand dunes in the Libyan desert.

99: RETROSPECTIVE REPORT

The quote has been encoded with a Caesar shift of +6. The full quote from Eppler is therefore: 'If I ever meet Almásy again, God, how I shall beat him up'.

In the end, however, Eppler never got to 'beat Almásy up'. Having made it back to Gialo safely, Almásy then returned to Hungary and wrote a book on his war deeds.

100: AN EXPENSIVE MISSION

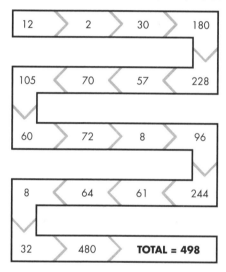

Jakobs was found with £498 – equivalent to over £20,000 in 2024.

101: WEATHERING THE STORM

Location	Day	Time	Conditions
Greenwich	Monday	Noon	Overcast
Richmond	Wednesday	7am	Drizzle
Ilford	Friday	9pm	Clear skies
Hampstead	Sunday	4pm	Hailstorm

102: LAST ON THE LIST

The words have been encoded with a shift of +10. The complete entries are therefore:

1. Country of birth: LUXEMBOURG
2. County of parachute landing: CAMBRIDGESHIRE
3. City Jakobs was ordered to send reports from: LONDON
4. Hospital where he was sent for surgery: DULWICH
5. Place of execution: TOWER OF LONDON

Jakobs bears the dubious distinction of being the last person ever to be put to death at the Tower of London.

103: A DOUBLE DECOY

The name of the decoy operation was BRIMSTONE. Additional words to find include: bent, besot, best, bestir, bet, bets, bistro, bit, bite, bites, bits, boniest, emit, emits, entomb, entombs, inert, inmost, insert, inset, inter, inters, into, intros, item, items, its, mentor, mentors, merit, merits, met, metro, metros, minster, mint, mints, mist, mite, mites, mitre, mitres, mobster, moist, moisten, moister, monster, mortise, most, mote, motes, nest, net, nets, nit, nitre, nits, not, note, notes, obit, obits, omit, omits, onset, orbit, orbits, orient, orients, remit, remits, rent, rents, rest, riot, riots, rite, rites, rot, rote, rotes, rots, sent, set, sit, site, smite, smote, snort, sort, sortie, sot, stein, stem, stern, stir, stone, stonier, store, storm, strobe, ten, tenor, tenors, tens, tensor, term, terms, tern, terns, tie, tier, tiers, ties, timber, timbers, timbre, timbres, time, timer, timers, times, tin, tine, tines, tins, tire, tires, toe, toes, tom, tomb, tombs, tome, tomes, toms, ton, tone, toner, tones, tonier, tons, tor, tore, torn, tors, tribe, tribes, tries, trim, trims, trio and trios.

104: THE MAN WHO NEVER WAS

The steps must be taken in the following order:

1. Create fake ID card
2. Forge letters
3. Invent family tree
4. Acquire false uniform
5. Buy cinema tickets
6. Cut bunch of keys
7. Take photo of 'wife'
8. Pack briefcase

105: IMPERSONAL EFFECTS

The words can be placed as follows:

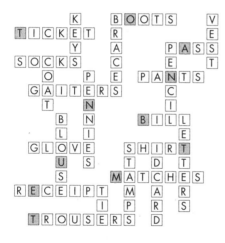

The highlighted letters can be rearranged to spell MOUNTBATTEN.

106: AN UNCANNY LIKENESS

The words are all names of major European cities, with one letter changed:

1. CAIRO – where Monty's double went into hiding after his false appearances.
2. LYON
3. RIGA
4. NICE
5. PRAGUE
6. PARIS
7. VIENNA
8. NAPLES

107: POTENTIAL PROJECTS

The names can be placed as follows:

The name which cannot be placed is CONGO – the name for the joint OSS and SOE Adriatic operations.

A list of codenames suggested by the Admiralty is shown below:

108: FRIENDLY FACT-FINDING

The units were mobilised in the following order:

1. E
2. B
3. F
4. C
5. A
6. H
7. G
8. D

109: JUST KEEPING TABS

Vehicle Type	Direction of Travel	Vehicle Count	Time of Day
Tank	East	8	12pm
Trailer	South	12	2pm
Train	West	4	7am
Pontoon	North	15	10am

110: THE BRIDGE OF SPIES

Your escape route should be as follows:

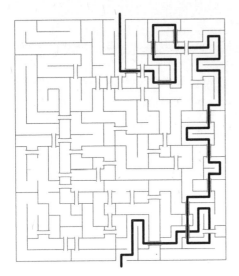

111: SUFFRAGETTE CODE

The entries can be tracked as follows:

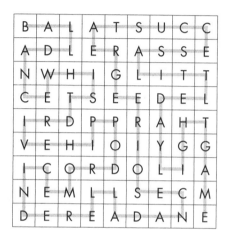

B	A	L	A	T	S	U	C	C
A	D	L	E	R	A	S	S	E
N	W	H	I	G	L	I	T	T
C	E	T	S	E	E	D	E	L
I	R	D	P	P	R	A	H	T
V	E	H	I	O	I	Y	G	G
I	C	O	R	D	O	L	I	A
N	E	M	L	L	S	E	C	M
D	E	R	E	A	D	A	N	E

The entries are therefore:

1. BALL
2. DANCE
3. WHIST DRIVE
4. HIPPODROME
5. CINDERELLA DANCE
6. SOIREE
7. GREAT SUCCESS
8. A LITTLE DAYLIGHT GAME

112: DEFT DEFINITION

A Caesar shift of +8 has been applied. The full passage therefore reads as follows:

> 'What is Code? Several DEFINITIONS have been used to DESCRIBE Code. It has been SPOKEN of as a DISGUISE; as a METHOD of CLOTHING words and SENTENCES so that only those with SPECIAL KNOWLEDGE can SEE through the DISGUISE; as the CLOAKING of INFORMATION so that only the INITIATED can PIERCE the VEIL.'

The full passage from the Postal Censorship guide, published in 1939, is shown here:

FOREWORD TO THE CODE SECTION

What is Code?

Several definitions have been used to describe Code. It has been spoken of as a disguise; as a method of clothing words and sentences so that only those with special knowledge can see through the disguise; as the cloaking of information so that only the initiated can pierce the veil.

Code dates from the earliest days, and every time it appears it has acquired new forms, for man's ingenuity continues to invent new ways of hiding things from the general public and revealing them to the chosen few.

In some countries Code is made the object of special study so that, if occasion arises, it can immediately be adopted for transmitting information between one country and another without the name of the sender or the information becoming known to any unauthorized person.

And when it is a question of finding out whether a document contains Code, or whether a letter covers more than meets the eye, there is immediately begun a battle of brains.

Imagination must be met by imagination, guile must be faced by guile. All possibilities must be considered and weighed with probabilities and improbabilities. And finally, it must be decided whether the verdict shall be guilty, or not guilty; whether the document contains Code or not.

And if, in the strivings between the examiner and the sender of the letter, the latter succeeds in baffling the former, let this only make him strive the harder not to allow himself to be baffled twice.

It is in order to minimize, as far as posible, the chances of Code escaping the examiner's eye that the following pages have been written.

113: SIGNED, SEALED, DECIPHERED

Stamp Value	Stamp Angle	Stamp Proximity	Secret Message
1d	Right way up	Touching 1 stamp	Troops on the move
½d	Sideways	Touching 2 stamps	Offensive imminent
2d	Upside down	Touching no stamps	Cover blown

114: PORTUGUESE PARAPHRASING

The words can be placed as follows:

	C	O	L	O	N	E	L	
	G	E	N	E	R	A	L	
	A	D	M	I	R	A	L	
F	A	C	T	O	R	I	E	S
F	O	R	T	R	E	S	S	
M	A	R	T	I	N			
H	U	R	R	I	C	A	N	E
A	E	R	O	D	R	O	M	E	S
	O	L	D	M	O	D	E	L
R	E	C	E	N	T	M	O	D	E	L
	S	P	I	T	F	I	R	E

The original list can be seen here:

Types of Planes

Martin
Flying Fortress
Consolidated
Hurricane
Spitfire
Boston Bomber
Wellington Bomber
Douglas
Recent model
Old model
Factories
General
Admiral
Colonel
Repair aerodromes
Aerodromes
The enemy's intentions
The difficulty of supplies
Contagious diseases
Hunger
Plans

remessa (remittance)
pimenta
Franco-Belga
Portuguese escudos
Angolares
Madeira
vinho branco (white wine)
vinho tinto (red wine)
preto, novo (black, new)
branco, velho (white, old)
azeite (oil)
milho (maize)
trigo (corn, wheat)
azeitonas (olives)
entrega
encargo (charge, duty)
vontade (will, desire)
dificil (difficult)
dificilimo (very difficult)
facil (easy)
intencoes (intentions)

115: NUMEROUS DISGUISES

In the substitution cipher, A = 6, B = 7, C = 8 and so on. The full quote therefore reads: 'NO WAR CAN BE CONDUCTED SUCCESSFULLY WITHOUT EARLY AND GOOD INTELLIGENCE'

116: COVERT CODES

Codename	Real name	Relationship	City
BERRY	Clive	Father	Melbourne
BLOSSOM	Sarah	Aunt	Washington DC
BUSH	Edwin	Cousin	Paris
BRACKEN	Eugenia	Sister	Tokyo

117: MIXED MEANINGS

The words can be unjumbled as follows:

HUT + B
HOTEL + U
FACTORY + I
HOUSE + L
MUSEUM + D
HOSPITAL + I
SCHOOL + N
CABIN + G

The theme which links the words is BUILDING.

118: THE RIGHT MESSAGE

Sent from	Code Type	Redacted Name	Sent to
Amsterdam	Anagrams	Monty	Oslo
London	Number Code	Blondie	Moscow
Toronto	Caesar Cipher	Reggie	Cairo
Cape Town	Underlined letters	Ziggy	Buenos Aires

119: CRACKING STUFF

The cities, and the shifts, are:

MANCHESTER, with a shift of 1
BLACKPOOL, with a shift of 2
NEWCASTLE, with a shift of 4
BIRMINGHAM, with a shift of 7
LONDON, with a shift of 11
LEEDS, with a shift of 16

The difference between one shift and the next increases by 1 each time. That is, the differences between successive shifts are 1, 2, 3, 4, 5 and so on.

120: DEUS EX MACHINA

Operation Codename	Sea Area	Number of Enemy Vessels
DODGE	Bailey	2
STRIFE	Sole	7
DART	Shannon	6
MIRAGE	Rockall	4

121: A NEW SYSTEM

The clues can be filled in as follows:

M	U	R	M	U	R	
A	I	R	M	A	N	
B	R	A	I	N	S	
M	I	N	I	M	U	M
B	A	R	B	A	R	I	A	N

The name of Turing's technique was therefore BANBURISMUS.

122: A SHORTER WAR

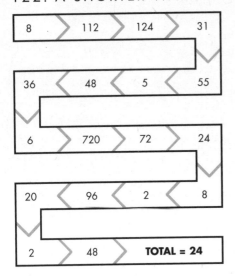

It is estimated that the war was shortened by 24 months – that is, two years.

123: HIGH PRAISE

The path can be traced as follows:

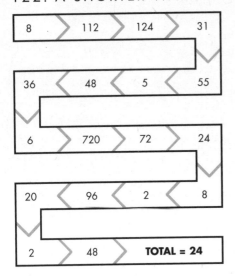

The alleged epithet for the workers of Bletchley Park is therefore 'THE GEESE WHO LAID THE GOLDEN EGGS AND NEVER CACKLED'.

124: THE PEN IS MIGHTIER

The reassembled items are:

CHOCOLATE
LEATHER BELT
SOAP
TALCUM POWDER
TOOTHPASTE TUBE
TORCH
WINE BOTTLE

125: UNFORESEEN DELAY

The devices are due to detonate in the following order of the spies'
codenames:

1. ASH
2. GRIZZLY
3. FOSS
4. NIMBUS
5. FROST
6. CUCKOO
7. TROUT
8. MAPLE

126: FALSE BOTTOMS

Carrier's Codename	Food in Tin	Hidden Device	Destination
AJAX	Beans	Detonator	Madrid
CLERK	Mash	Primer	Bordeaux
MISTER	Pie	Igniter	Coventry

127: NOT SO SWEET

The sweets and weapons can be separated as follows:

MINT + SWORD
BONBON + RIFLE
GUMDROP + PISTOL
NOUGAT + TORPEDO
CARAMEL + ROCKET
LOLLIPOP + MISSILE
LOZENGE + CANNON
SHERBET + DAGGER
BUTTERSCOTCH + CATAPULT
HUMBUG + MUSKET

128: A CURIOUS CASE

Briefcase Colour	Agent's Nationality	Destination
Red	Finnish	Antwerp
Brown	French	Limoges
Black	German	Barcelona
Blue	Portuguese	Copenhagen

129: CANNED BADS

The French dish is CASSOULET. Its name can be seen on the can of a disguised incendiary device in the image opposite:

Other words to find include: aces, acts, acutes, ales, aloes, also, altos, ascot, ascots, ass, asset, autos, case, cases, cast, caste, castes, castle, castles, casts, cats, cause, causes, class, clause, clauses, cleats, close, closes, closest, closet, closets, clots, clouts, clues, coals, coast, coasts, coats, cols, colts, cost, costs, cotes, cots, cues, cults, cutlass, cuts, east, eats, laces, lactose, lass, last, lasts, lats, leas, least, less, lest, lets, locates, locus, locust, locusts, lose, loses, loss, lost, lots, lotus, lotuses, louse, louses, louts, lust, lusts, lutes, oases, oust, ousts, outclass, outs, sac, sacs, sale, sales, salt, salts, salute, salutes, sat, sate, sates, sauce, sauces, saute, sautes, scale, scales, scout, scouts, sea, seal, seals, seas, seat, seats, sect, sects, set, sets, slat, slate, slates, slats, sloe, slot, slots, sol, solace, solaces, sole, soles, sols, sot, sots, soul, souls, souse, stale, stales, steal, steals, stole, stoles, sue, sues, suet, tacos, taels, tales, tassel, teals, teas, toes, toss, tousle, tousles, tussle, use and uses.

130: HIDDEN WIRES

The items can be found as follows:

P	A	I	N	O	X	B	A
B	R	A	T	B	R	H	T
A	T	C	S	E	O	O	M
E	T	F	T	L	A	C	S
R	R	I	W	O	O	D	G
Y	D	H	P	O	M	A	R
E	N	O	U	M	E	A	N
V	A	C	U	C	L	R	E

The items which could have been used to hide wireless equipment are therefore:

PAINT BOX
BATHROOM SCALES
CAR BATTERY
DRIFTWOOD
GRAMOPHONE
VACUUM CLEANER

An explanation of how wireless sets were camouflaged from the SOE training manual.

131: THE WIRELESS DEPARTMENT

The Morse code can be decoded as follows:

TOULOUSE   ATHENS
ROME   ALMERIA
AARHUS   OSLO
MILAN   MARSEILLE
LILLE

132: TIME TO NAME NAMES

Codename	Training Name	Field Name	Location
NECKING	TAZELAAR	TONY	Friesland
SCRAPE	SCHEFFER	VICTOR	Rotterdam
SPLASH	PALSTRA	JIM	Amsterdam
WHIMPER	BENDER	FRED	Veluwe

133: CONVINCING FAKES

Agent Codename	Document Type	Document Category	Destination
FLANNEL	Identity card	Essential	The Hague
SPANNER	False transfer papers	Emergency	Rotterdam
CRUX	Theatre ticket	Corroborative	Utrecht

134: MULTIPLE IDENTITIES

The names can be placed as follows:

NOTES